YORK NOTES

General Editors: Professor A.N. Jeffares (University of Stirling) & Professor Suheil Bushrui (American University of Beirut)

William Thackeray

VANITY FAIR

Notes by Harry Edmund Shaw

BA (HARVARD) MA PH D (BERKELEY, CALIFORNIA)
Assistant Professor, Cornell University

LONGMAN
YORK PRESS

YORK PRESS
Immeuble Esseily, Place Riad Solh, Beirut.

LONGMAN GROUP LIMITED
Longman House, Burnt Mill, Harlow
Essex CM20 2JE, England
Associated companies throughout the world

First published 1980
Second impression 1984
ISBN 0 582 78102 7
Printed in Hong Kong by
Sing Cheong Printing Co Ltd

Part 1

Introduction

POLITICAL CHANGE and economic growth, the spread of cities, the explosive, transforming power of technological discoveries—these are things which modern men and women in most parts of the world have come to take for granted. But they have not always been the norm. They first made themselves felt in full strength during the nineteenth century, particularly in England but also in Western Europe. It must have been a confusing time in which to live. The industrial revolution was transforming centuries-old patterns of social organisation and work, and indeed the very landscape. Cities grew where there had been only villages before. The French Revolution and its Napoleonic aftermath provided unsettling glimpses of the possibility of mass political change on a scale hitherto hardly imagined.

We can think of novels like Thackeray's *Vanity Fair* as attempts to see and understand this changing society. If we compare a great eighteenth-century novel, Fielding's *Tom Jones* for instance, with the best works of Dickens or Thackeray or George Eliot, one thing that stands out unmistakably about the nineteenth-century novels is that they give a much denser, more specific and detailed picture of the societies in which they are set. The portrait is not complete. The attempt to capture the working class in nineteenth-century fiction is a series of honourable failures, and some novels, *Vanity Fair* among them, do not even try. The ultimate aim of such novels is also likely to transcend the depiction of contemporary society. Nonetheless, one of the attractions of a novel such as *Vanity Fair* for contemporary readers must have been the way in which it at least seemed to give a broad, panoramic view of a society which was becoming ever more difficult to understand.

William Makepeace Thackeray (1811–63) was in many respects well situated to give a picture of the middle and upper classes in nineteenth-century England. Socially, he was both an insider and an outsider, which gave him both knowledge of and distance from the society he portrayed. He came from a wealthy family, which sent him to school at Charterhouse and to the University of Cambridge, after which he travelled to Weimar, the 'Pumpernickel' of *Vanity Fair*. All of this makes him sound as if he were a typical son of a prosperous British upper-middle-class family. But his parents were not simply British, they were (like Jos in *Vanity Fair*) Anglo-Indians. A successful member of the British civil service in India could accumulate a good deal of money in a relatively short time, if only his health stood up to the severe climate. Even when they returned to England, the Anglo-Indians tended to form their own society, partly because they had formed similar habits during their service abroad, partly because normal British society tended to distrust them as members of a newly wealthy class.

In 1833, Thackeray lost the small fortune he had inherited. After leaving Cambridge he had worked in the law and in finance; now he decided to become a painter, which led him to Paris. There he met and in 1836 married Isabella Shawe. Having realised that he would never be a successful painter, he returned to England, intent on making his fortune as a writer. He contributed to several periodicals; increasingly successful, he devoted himself with increasing single-mindedness to his work. This led him to neglect his wife. She was never a strong and stable person, and the various strains in her life finally proved too much for her. She felt unable to run Thackeray's house efficiently or to share his intellectual interests; in 1840, she attempted suicide. Not long after she became incurably insane, reverting to the mental level of a child.

During the early 1840s, Thackeray continued to write prolifically. In 1844, he began a series entitled 'Pen and Pencil Sketches of English Society', but dropped it in favour of other projects. In 1846 he returned to the chapters he had written, revised them, and 'Pen and Pencil Sketches of English Society' became *Vanity Fair*. During the next decade he produced his greatest novels, including *Vanity Fair, Pendennis, Henry Esmond*, and *The Newcomes*. Thackeray wrote actively until the end of his life. He died in 1863.

Like most of the other great nineteenth-century English novels, *Vanity Fair* originally appeared in serial form. It was published in monthly parts or 'numbers' over a period of nineteen months, from January 1847 to July 1848. The final number was, according to customary practice, double the normal length, and thus there are twenty parts in all. Like Dickens, Thackeray wrote his novel as it was being published. Serial publication creates a particularly close relationship between audience and author. The author can see how his story is being received as he writes it. Readers have actually tried to influence the outcome of such works: the classic case involves Charles Dickens, who received anguished letters pleading with him not to kill off one of his characters, Little Nell, in the next number of *The Old Curiosity Shop*. (He did anyway.) Such reactions are extreme, but not really surprising. A story which is read bit by bit, not in a few days or weeks but over a period of several years, gains a peculiar reality. A reader feels that he or she has been living with the characters. The special kind of reality which serial publication promotes may help to explain a narrative peculiarity in *Vanity Fair*. Toward the end of the novel, the narrator tells us that he met the main characters in the novel personally in the German town of Pumpernickel, just as you or I might meet someone on a vacation. This is certainly an extreme case of treating fictional characters as if they were real people.

It is also worth pointing out that Thackeray drew numerous illustrations for his text. (Some modern editions reproduce these in part or completely, others do not.) Some of the illustrations have the effect of providing yet another layer of commentary on the action of the novel. The final full-page picture, for instance, gives a version of Dobbin and Amelia happening upon Becky at the charity bazaar which is different in detail from the description of the meeting in the novel itself. Amelia's little daughter seems to want to buy something from Becky in the drawing, whereas in the novel what is described is 'the Colonel seizing up his little Janey' and presumably hustling her away.

A more striking example of the importance of Thackeray's drawings involves Jos's death. Thackeray strengthens the hint that Becky may have murdered Jos with an illustration entitled 'Becky's second appearance in the character of Clytemnestra', which depicts Becky grimly clutching something (is it poison?) in her hand, as she hides behind a curtain and overhears the conversation in which Jos begs Dobbin to come to live near him and protect him from her. In Greek legend, Clytemnestra murdered her husband Agamemnon. Becky's first appearance in the role occurs during a set of elaborate charades performed at one of Lord Steyne's parties.

Vanity Fair first appeared in book form in 1848. There was a revised version in 1853, and it has been reprinted many times since.

When *Vanity Fair* first appeared, some readers were surprised at its depth and seriousness. They were more familiar with Thackeray as a writer of comic prose and a satirist who pointed out some of the absurdities and weaknesses of his society. His early works are full of literary parody, in which he mimics and makes fun of the styles of other authors. Some of this side of Thackeray can be seen in *Vanity Fair* itself. He begins Chapter 6, which describes the trip to Vauxhall, with comments on how different kinds of popular novelists might handle the material he is about to present. Our early glimpses of Sir Pitt Crawley are also particularly amusing if we recognise certain literary conventions and stereotypes which Thackeray is parodying. Becky mistakes Sir Pitt for a porter because of his slovenly dress and vulgar accent. He is certainly not, as Becky remarks in one of her letters to Amelia Sedley, the sort of nobleman who appears in many eighteenth-century novels, since he is neither young, polite, generous, nor handsome. Further parody occurs in Becky's letters themselves, this time at the expense of the great eighteenth-century novelist Samuel Richardson (1689–1761), who invented the 'epistolatory novel' (a novel in which the narration takes the form of letters). In a famous scene in Richardson's first work, *Pamela*, the heroine breaks off her letter abruptly and then resumes to write that a wicked nobleman has just interrupted her as she was writing in her bedroom and made sexual advances to her. Becky interrupts a letter too, but in her case the wicked nobleman has burst into her room for a purpose that is not sexual but economic. Sir Pitt makes her put out her candle, since candles cost money.

These early scenes provide comic entertainment. But as the novel progresses, Thackeray's reference to other works of literature ceases to be mere parody and becomes a serious criticism. In the scene in which Dobbin tells Amelia that she is unworthy of him, Thackeray does not simply upset our conventional expectations about how men and women in novels act, he asks us to consider how such conventional feelings and ideals may have helped to *make* Amelia unworthy of Dobbin—or may distort our own values. In *Vanity Fair*, Thackeray comes into his own: he becomes a profound commentator on society and on life.

A note on the text

Vanity Fair appeared in twenty separately published monthly parts, the last two issued together, from January 1847 to July 1848; included were thirty-eight full-page drawings and numerous smaller drawings and decorations, drawn by Thackeray himself. The novel first appeared in book form in 1848 and a revised version in 1853, published by Bradbury and Evans, London. Two carefully annotated, reliably edited texts of *Vanity Fair* with good introductions are presently available in paperback, one edited by J. I. M. Stewart, Penguin Books, Harmondsworth, 1968, the other edited by Geoffrey and Kathleen Tillotson, Houghton Mifflin, Boston, 1963. The Tillotson edition contains all of Thackeray's full-page illustrations and a few of his smaller drawings; the Stewart edition has only one but gives very full notes. For a look at all of the drawings, the student should consult one of the better collected editions of Thackeray's works, such as the one edited by George Saintsbury, Oxford University Press, London, 1908. The text used in the preparation of these notes has been the edition by J. I. M. Stewart, Penguin Books, Harmondsworth, 1968.

Part 2

Summaries

of VANITY FAIR

A general summary

Vanity Fair follows the lives of two schoolmates, Becky Sharp and Amelia Sedley. Amelia comes from a well-to-do family. She is simple, gentle, and loving. Becky is intelligent, energetic, resilient, and poor. As soon as she leaves school, Becky begins a series of attempts to reach social eminence and financial security. She tries to ensnare Amelia's brother Jos as a husband, but fails. Then she becomes a governess in the family of Sir Pitt Crawley, making herself so agreeable that Sir Pitt finally proposes to her. Unfortunately for Becky she had already secretly married Sir Pitt's younger son, Rawdon, who is an army officer. When the family learn of this, Rawdon is disinherited.

Amelia meanwhile has spent her time dreaming about the day when she will marry George Osborne; they have been promised to each other for years. But Mr Sedley's business fails, the family is reduced to poverty, and old Mr Osborne forbids the marriage. George, who is selfish and unworthy of Amelia's love, seems ready to agree with his father, but his friend and fellow army officer William Dobbin persuades him to act more honourably. George marries Amelia, and his father promptly disinherits him.

The two young couples meet in Brussels, where the English army has arrived to fight Napoleon. Becky flirts with George, who is so infatuated with her that he writes her a letter begging her to run off with him. But the Battle of Waterloo intervenes, and he is killed.

Amelia returns to England, where she gives birth to a son. Her financial situation grows so precarious that she is forced to hand over her young son, George, to his grandfather, old Mr Osborne. He still refuses to have anything to do with her, except to support her and her parents. Becky meanwhile has succeeded in climbing to the top of the social ladder in London. She still does not have any money, but her wit and charm attract the powerful nobleman Lord Steyne, from whom she obtains money and an entrée into the highest society. Her husband Rawdon does not realise that she has been taking money from Steyne. One day Rawdon is arrested for debt, and Becky does nothing to help him. He is able to gain his freedom anyway, and returns home that evening only to find Steyne and Becky alone together. Rawdon strikes down Steyne as he tries to leave, and vows never to see Becky again. Steyne also never forgives her for this scene. She is a ruined woman. An outcast from English society, she goes to the Continent, where she moves from place to place in search of a social set that will accept her.

As Becky's fortunes fall, Amelia's rise. Her brother Jos had been in India; now he returns and supports Amelia and her parents in a grand style. Old Osborne dies, and Amelia's son George is restored to her. William Dobbin has been in love with Amelia for years, but she refuses to marry him, thinking that she should remain faithful to her dead husband.

Jos, Amelia, and Dobbin take a trip to the Continent, where they happen to meet Becky. She reveals that George had wanted to run off with her before Waterloo. Amelia now realises that George was not worthy of her devotion, and she feels free to marry Dobbin. They return to England, but Jos stays behind. Becky is soon able to gain complete control over him and his finances. He dies, and Becky returns to England, using Jos's money to gain at least a semi-respectable place in society.

The title

Thackeray takes his title from *The Pilgrim's Progress* (1678), an allegory by John Bunyan (1628–88), which describes a physical journey that stands for man's spiritual journey through life. In this work, 'Vanity Fair' is in literal terms a fair, a place where goods are sold and people are entertained. In allegorical terms, 'Vanity Fair' stands for human society, with its vain concern for pleasure and material objects, the things which one goes to a fair to obtain. This, Thackeray would seem to be saying, is the sort of world his characters inhabit.

Detailed summaries

Chapter 1: Chiswick Mall

Vanity Fair opens as two of the novel's principal characters are about to leave school and enter the adult world, the 'Vanity Fair' of the novel's title. Amelia Sedley is the daughter of a prosperous London merchant. Everyone connected with the boarding school is sorry to see her go. She is gentle, good-natured, pretty, easily moved to tears, and moderately intelligent. She embodies, in short, one nineteenth-century ideal of femininity.

The other girl who is leaving Miss Pinkerton's academy is very different from Amelia Sedley. Becky Sharp was not a fee-paying student. Instead, she was a kind of servant. An orphan whose father used to give drawing lessons for Miss Pinkerton's pupils before he died, Becky was allowed food, lodging, some tuition, and a very small salary in return for speaking French with the younger girls in the school. (She learned the language from her French mother, who had been an opera dancer, a very disreputable profession in the nineteenth century.) Amelia has invited Becky home with her for a short visit before Becky becomes a governess to a noble family.

Thackeray uses the action of the opening chapters to throw into sharp relief the difference between Becky and Amelia. The most graphic example of this involves Johnson's *Dictionary*, the book which Miss Pinkerton traditionally gives to her pupils when they leave the academy. Miss Pinkerton presents the *Dictionary* to Amelia, who accepts it gratefully. She offers nothing to Becky Sharp. Miss Pinkerton loathes Becky, who had earlier refused to teach music at the academy unless she was paid extra for doing so. Becky hates Miss Pinkerton because she values her students according to their financial means, not their intelligence, which puts Becky at the bottom of the scale. Becky has revenged herself on Miss Pinkerton in a variety of ways, among them by speaking French to her. The old lady cannot understand the language, but is embarrassed to admit it.

It is no surprise, then, that Miss Pinkerton does not even consider giving Becky her traditional parting gift of Johnson's *Dictionary*. But Miss Pinkerton has a sister, the kindly, rather stupid Jemima Pinkerton, who is naive enough to think that poor Becky will be crushed if she does not receive the book. Jemima first tries to persuade her sister to give the *Dictionary* to Becky. Of course she fails, but her misdirected, admirable, amusing concern for Becky's feelings causes her to summon up enough courage to steal a copy from her sister's office. She gives it to Becky on the sly, as Becky enters the coach that will carry her and Amelia to Amelia's home. Becky's response is typical. While Amelia is filled with warm, happy thoughts about Miss Pinkerton's academy and her years there, Becky defiantly flings the *Dictionary* back into the courtyard as the coach drives away.

NOTES AND GLOSSARY:

Semiramis:	a wise Assyrian princess; the comparison is meant to belittle Miss Pinkerton
Dr Johnson:	eminent man of letters (1709–84); published his *Dictionary* in 1755
Mrs Chapone:	(1727–1801) wrote a work on education

Mrs Billington:	a famous opera singer of the day. Throughout *Vanity Fair*, Thackeray refers to singers, dancers, actors, boxers, and the like who were active during the times in which the novel is set
round-hand:	a style of handwriting taught at schools

Chapter 2: In which Miss Sharp and Miss Sedley Prepare to Open the Campaign

As the carriage rolls on, Becky's excitement at having openly defied Miss Pinkerton leads her to another expression of social defiance. When she screams out '*Vive la France! Vive l'Empereur! Vive Bonaparte!*', she is being very daring indeed, since, as the narrator tells us, during the time in which the novel is set, England was engaged in a war with Napoleon, who was viewed by conservative public opinion as the devil himself. Becky's enthusiasm is primarily motivated by a desire to be as shocking and rebellious as possible, but her outburst also has a larger significance. Becky wants to be a kind of Napoleon herself: she wants to scale the social heights as he has scaled the political heights. The parallel has its ironies. For all his lowly origins and republican beginnings, Napoleon at last threw his lot in with the upper classes and became an Emperor. For all her rebelliousness, it is clear enough that Becky will have to achieve her rise in a similar way. She has already started on this path by getting herself invited to Amelia's home as well as coercing Miss Pinkerton into finding her a job as a governess in an aristocratic family.

Thus as the two girls leave Miss Pinkerton's academy, they entertain very different thoughts. Amelia feels sad to have left her friends, but is also excited to be entering a new life. Becky is less sentimental. Her principal concern, now and throughout the novel, is to be sure that she takes advantage of every opportunity to climb the social ladder and escape her poverty and dependence on the whims of others.

NOTES AND GLOSSARY:

Dr Raine:	Headmaster of Charterhouse 1791–1811
'*Vive la France!* ....:'	(*French*) Long live France! Long live the Emperor! Long live Bonaparte!
Mr Lawrence:	Sir Thomas Lawrence (1769–1830) was a famous painter, as was Benjamin West (1738–1820)
Minerva:	Greek goddess of wisdom, ironically compared to Miss Pinkerton

Chapter 3: Rebecca is in Presence of the Enemy

For a girl in Becky Sharp's position, the only practical way to better her status is to find a man who is willing to marry her and to rise by means of him. Becky has attempted this feat once already in her short life, with a young clergyman who visited Miss Pinkerton's academy. She nearly succeeded, but Miss Pinkerton discovered and put a stop to the budding affair. A second chance presents itself to Becky when she arrives at Amelia's home, in the bulky figure of Amelia's brother Joseph (or Jos) Sedley, home on leave from his job in the East India Company's civil service in India. Becky decides to ensnare him. Jos, however, is a coward, especially where women are concerned. Capturing *him*, the narrator tells us, will be no easy task even for Becky.

NOTES AND GLOSSARY:
Billingsgate: London fish-market
bon-vivant: (*French*) one who enjoys good food and drink

Chapter 4: The Green Silk Purse

Becky nearly succeeds in her aim; she makes Jos believe that she is fascinated by him and by India. In general, Becky is on her best behaviour with the Sedleys, smiling in return for Mr Sedley's crude practical jokes, ingratiating herself with Mrs Sedley and even with the servants, refusing to be separated from Amelia when Amelia falls ill one afternoon. Perhaps her most cunning ploy is to sing a mournful song about a poor orphan about to leave her friends. She seems so emotionally affected that she cannot finish the song. The Sedleys remember that she is an orphan, and her stay with them is extended.

While all of this is going on, we learn about another love affair. Amelia and George Osborne have been intended for each other by their parents since the two of them were children, and they are very much in love—at least Amelia is in love with George. George is mainly in love with himself, as Becky Sharp with her quick intelligence realises from seeing him glance at himself approvingly in the mirror.

Jos is almost on the point of proposing to Becky, who gives him every opportunity to do so, but he cannot quite bring himself to take such a dramatic step. Then a trip for the two couples is planned. They will visit Vauxhall, the London park where Jos decides he will propose to Becky.

NOTES AND GLOSSARY:
Exeter 'Change: Exeter Exchange, where there was a circus noted for its elephant

Boney: derisive British name for Napoleon

a grand allegorical title: George is thinking of books which depict on their title-pages allegorical figures, such as a woman meant to represent Truth or Virtue

mahout: elephant driver

Sehnsucht nach der Liebe: (*German*) 'longing for love'

after Cutchery: after Jos has come home for the day from his duties as an Indian magistrate

tiffin: (*Anglo-Indian*) luncheon

Chapter 5: Dobbin of Ours

Will the timid Jos actually propose to Becky? For the moment, Thackeray leaves us in suspense. He breaks the narrative line to introduce a major character whom we have not yet encountered, William Dobbin, and to give us additional insight into George Osborne's character. Thackeray goes back in time to describe the lives of the two men at school. Dobbin was an awkward boy, whom the other students despised for his low class status. His father was a tradesman, and he paid for Dobbin's schooling not with money but with goods. This seemed unspeakably vulgar to the other students, who were sons of gentlemen and in some cases of the nobility.

Dobbin had a miserable time at school until a dramatic event took place. For some reason, he was fond of George Osborne. One day, the most influential and respected boy in the school (who was also a bit of a bully and tyrannised over younger, weaker boys), was in the process of beating George, who had displeased him. Dobbin became enraged and challenged the bully to a fist fight. To the amazement of all, he won, and from that time his situation in the school changed completely. Where he had been jeered at, now he was respected and well treated.

George Osborne's part in the whole affair is revealing. He, it turns out, was the one who had originally let the other boys know that Dobbin's fees were paid in goods and not in money. He was initially embarrassed to have a lower-class boy defend him; after Dobbin became popular, George patronised him and condescended to him. Dobbin for his part continued to idolise George for no very clear reason; so do most other people, including George's own family and Amelia Sedley.

In the years that have passed since his schooldays, Dobbin's social position has altered greatly. His father has become rich and been knighted. Dobbin himself has entered the army, and George Osborne is a member of the same army unit.

George sees to it that Dobbin is invited to the party at Vauxhall (and here we rejoin the main line of the story). When Dobbin arrives at the Sedleys, he is much struck by Amelia's beauty, an impression which is to ripen and prove of the greatest importance as the novel proceeds. As the party gets ready to leave for Vauxhall, Jos pours down drink after drink. It is obvious to everyone that he is trying to work up the courage to propose to Becky. But the question remains—will he be able to bring himself to do so?

NOTES AND GLOSSARY:
Bell's Life: a newspaper which covered sporting events

Chapter 6: Vauxhall

As it turns out, Jos does not propose to Becky. Two things prevent him from proposing. First, he orders a peculiarly strong drink at Vauxhall called 'rack punch', and becomes utterly and loudly drunk, so that he is in no state to propose to anyone, though he does sing songs and shout, to the vast amusement of the other visitors to Vauxhall. Any remaining chance that he will propose to Becky is destroyed the next morning, by George Osborne. George is a snob. He expects to marry Amelia, and he objects to having a governess as a sister-in-law. So he visits Jos's lodgings and ridicules him for his behaviour at Vauxhall, suggesting among other things that Becky might sue him for breach of promise of marriage. George knows very well that the sensitive Jos will drop any thought of pursuing Becky after these cruel comments, and he is right. Jos leaves London immediately.

George then goes to Amelia's house, where he jokes about Jos's hangover. Becky Sharp realises from George's mocking tone that he has probably ruined her chances of marrying Jos by embarrassing him about his conduct at Vauxhall. George does not know it, but he has made an enemy.

NOTES AND GLOSSARY:
Vauxhall: famous public gardens, originally laid out in the seventeenth century and much frequented by Londoners
the Corsican Upstart: Napoleon
Daniel Lambert: (1770-1809) a famous fat man of the day
Sister Anne: she was on the watch-tower awaiting the arrival of help against her murderous husband Bluebeard

Chapter 7: Crawley of Queen's Crawley

Becky is now in an awkward position. There is nothing to do but to leave the Sedleys and take up her position as governess to the family of Sir Pitt Crawley, Baronet. Becky expects him to be like the handsome, refined noblemen she has read about in novels. When she arrives at his house in London, where she is to meet him before going to his country house in Hampshire, she makes a discovery. Becky is met by a rude, shabbily dressed man with a provincial accent, and she assumes that he is the butler. In fact, it turns out that he is Sir Pitt himself.

NOTES AND GLOSSARY:

Jack Sheppard: a famous highwayman or robber, hanged in 1724
old Weller: Tony Weller, a coach-driver who appears in *The Pickwick Papers* (1836-7) by Charles Dickens (1812-70)

Chapter 8: Private and Confidential

The next section of the novel deals with Becky's life with the family of Sir Pitt Crawley, who live in the country in Hampshire, south of London. Throughout these chapters, Thackeray has great fun in exploding the idea that country life brings with it an 'Arcadian' simplicity and contentment. He shows that life in Hampshire is instead just as corrupt, grasping, and riddled with snobbishness as life in London.

Sir Pitt is an energetic, selfish, stingy man with a provincial accent. His brother Bute is a 'type' character familiar in English fiction—the hunting parson. He prefers horse-riding and hunting to preaching. His more intelligent wife, 'Mrs Bute', writes his sermons for him. He and Sir Pitt are constantly feuding.

NOTES AND GLOSSARY:

Cecilia: a novel of high society by Fanny Burney (1752-1840)
Lord Orville: hero of another Burney novel, *Evelina*
castle of Udolpho: the main setting for the Gothic novel *The Mysteries of Udolpho* (1794), by Ann Radcliffe (1764-1823)
Mouton aux navets:(*French*) 'mutton and turnips'; this and the following French phrases are fancy names for plain food

Chapter 9: Family Portraits

Sir Pitt has four children, two sons by his first wife (who died some time ago) and a pair of girls by his second wife, a completely insignificant though pitiable character who dies during Becky Sharp's tenure as governess. The sons could not be more different from one another. The older son, Pitt Crawley, is stern and reserved. Since he is a Methodist, he disapproves of gaming of any kind, drinking, and most of the other things which his father enjoys. Pitt's brother, Rawdon Crawley, is very different. He is an officer in the army, an expert gamesman and gambler, handsome, worldly, profane in language, and considerably less intelligent than his studious brother.

NOTES AND GLOSSARY:

'alieni ... profusus':(*Latin*, from Sallust, *Cataline* 5), 'He coveted other people's money and wasted his own'

Debrett: *Debrett's Peerage* lists the titled families of Great Britain

an Independent meeting house: as a Methodist, he does not attend the Church of England parish church of which Bute Crawley is rector

Chapter 10: Miss Sharp Begins to Make Friends

As her stay with the Crawley family progresses, Becky ingratiates herself with everyone. She helps Sir Pitt with his paperwork and the lawsuits that he loves. She listens to Pitt's sermons and reads his tracts. She sees a good deal of Rawdon Crawley, and he becomes increasingly fascinated by her. In Chapter 11, Mrs. Bute Crawley does what she can to forward this relationship, for reasons which are as yet unclear.

NOTES AND GLOSSARY:

Smollett: Tobias Smollett (1721-71) wrote histories and novels; despite its name, *The History of Humphrey Clinker* is one of the latter. Henry Fielding (1707-54) also wrote novels, as did Crébillon (1707-77) and Voltaire (1694-1778)

D'Hozier's dictionary: deals with the family trees of the French nobility; Becky has used it to construct a fictitious family for herself

Chapter 11: Arcadian Simplicity

A major event occurs, when another member of the Crawley family visits Sir Pitt at his Hampshire estate. This is Sir Pitt's half-sister, Miss Crawley, an unmarried, elderly woman who is an object of great interest and respect to her relatives because she happens to be very wealthy. She has stated that she will leave half of her fortune to Rawdon Crawley and half to Bute Crawley and his family. She despises Pitt Crawley's religiosity, since she herself enjoys eating, drinking, gambling, and all of the other genteel vices of the rich and sophisticated.

Becky is successful in making friends with Miss Crawley too. In fact, she succeeds so well that in Chapter 14 Miss Crawley demands that Sir Pitt allow Becky to accompany her to her home in London, after she is taken ill with a case of indigestion so severe that it almost kills her. Becky finds herself nursing Miss Crawley, who is a most unpleasant patient.

Becky has thus done rather well for herself during the year she has spent with the Crawleys. Miss Crawley finds her indispensable, and Sir Pitt, Rawdon, and Pitt Crawley all admire her intensely. Just how successful she has been with certain male members of the family we shall learn in due course.

NOTES AND GLOSSARY:

Arcadian: refers to a region of Greece which in literary convention is associated with a simple and good country life, free from the vices and cares of the city

---

Chapter 12: Quite a Sentimental Chapter

Amelia Sedley meanwhile devotes all of her energy to dreaming about George Osborne and trying to please him, and why not? Their fathers have intended the two to marry ever since they were children.

NOTES AND GLOSSARY:

the Foundling: a London orphanage; the chapel there
Iachimo: a villain in Shakespeare's *Cymbeline*; he crept into the heroine's chamber and stole a ring from her
Moonshine appears in Shakespeare's *A Midsummer Night's Dream*

Chapter 13: Sentimental and Otherwise

All is not well with Amelia. George's sisters domineer over her and patronise her, treating her as if she were not their equal, and they constantly tell George, who seems to believe them, that Amelia is not worthy of him. It becomes increasingly clear that George Osborne is vain and selfish. He neglects Amelia. When his sisters believe that he is visiting her, he is often amusing himself with other young officers instead. George is no match for the men with whom he associates. Among them is Rawdon Crawley, who is delighted to relieve George of his father's money at billiards or cards.

Even graver problems loom ahead for Amelia. Her father's business is on the brink of failure. She does not realise this, but Mr Osborne does. When she visits the Osbornes for dinner, he frowns at her and is all but openly rude. He tells his son that night that even though he owes his own financial success to Mr Sedley, he is not going to allow George to marry a pauper. If Mr Sedley cannot provide a suitable dowry, George must look elsewhere for a wife. George says nothing, but when he rejoins Amelia he is particularly attentive to her.

NOTES AND GLOSSARY:

Admirable Crichton: James Crichton (*c*.1560-85) was a Scotsman whose learning reached almost legendary proportions, particularly in foreign languages

Iphigenia: in Greek legend, she was sacrificed by her father Agamemnon, to procure a favourable wind for the naval expedition against Troy. Amelia, too, is doomed to be sacrificed, not by her own father but by George's

---

Chapter 14: Miss Crawley at Home

Becky remains in London even after Miss Crawley recovers from her illness. She sees a good deal of Rawdon Crawley and makes a fool of George Osborne when the latter visits Miss Crawley's house and tries to patronise her.

In the closing pages of the chapter occurs a memorable scene. Sir Pitt's wife has died, and he comes up to London to visit Becky. He implores her to come back to his country home in Hampshire. When she hesitates, he takes the amazing step of asking her, penniless governess though she is, to marry him. The scene of Sir Pitt Crawley, Baronet, on his knees before Becky, leering at her in frustrated desire, is unforgettable. So is her answer—that she is married already!

NOTES AND GLOSSARY:

Dives: the rich man in the biblical parable who refuses to help the beggar Lazarus (Luke 16); the name is used to refer to rich people in general

Croesus: the last, fabulously wealthy king of Lydia (560-546BC). Like Dives, he came to a bad end, being conquered by Cyrus, King of Persia

Chapter 15: In which Rebecca's Husband Appears for a Short Time

Becky manages for the time being not to tell anyone the name of the person she has married. It is in fact Rawdon Crawley, and Becky is justifiably worried that the family will disown him for marrying a woman without money. She wants to break the news in the right way.

NOTES AND GLOSSARY:

Pigault le Brun: a French writer of licentious novels (1753-1835)

Chapter 16: The Letter on the Pincushion

Becky finally decides to leave Miss Crawley's house and join Rawdon. She leaves a note explaining that she has married Rawdon. It is addressed to Briggs, Miss Crawley's companion, who Becky hopes will break the news gently to Miss Crawley. This is a mistake, since Briggs is jealous of Becky, who had taken over her own function when she nursed Miss Crawley through her sickness. Things are made worse for Becky by the arrival of Mrs Bute Crawley, who has learned of Becky's marriage and has a good idea of the identity of the groom, since she did her best to promote the match back in Hampshire. The Bute Crawleys hope to inherit all of Miss Crawley's money should she disown Rawdon. Thus Miss Crawley learns that Becky has married Rawdon from two of Becky's worst enemies.

Meanwhile Becky and Rawdon wait to see what Miss Crawley will do. Becky decides that even if Miss Crawley does indeed disown them, she herself will make their fortune through her own energy and intelligence.

NOTES AND GLOSSARY:

Achilles and Ajax: two Greek heroes in the *Iliad*

Hercules: a Greek hero who was punished for committing murder by being made the slave for a year of Omphale, Queen of Lydia: she made him do women's work

Samson: the Bible records how Samson revealed to Delilah that the secret of his strength lay in his hair. She cut it off, and his enemies enslaved him (Judges 13-16)

Chapter 17: How Captain Dobbin Bought a Piano

This chapter opens at an auction. For a while, Thackeray playfully neglects to inform the reader whose goods are being auctioned off, but it becomes apparent that Mr Sedley is a bankrupt and that his goods are being disposed of. Captain Dobbin is there. He buys Amelia's piano and sends it to her, allowing her to think that George Osborne had done this for her. Rawdon Crawley and his new wife, Becky, also happen to drop by. As a joke, they buy a picture of Jos Sedley riding an elephant, and they bid against Dobbin for the piano. Rawdon remarks to Becky that Amelia is going to lose her prospective husband as well as her fortune, since old Mr Osborne will not allow his son to marry a penniless girl. Becky smilingly says that Amelia will get over her sorrow.

Rawdon is right about Mr Osborne. He has been the most merciless of Mr Sedley's creditors. He wants to forget all that Mr Sedley had done for him when they were both young men, and he has no intention of allowing his son to marry Amelia now that she is poor. Thus Mr Osborne needs to convince himself that Sedley is a cheat and a villain—that his recent actions have been so bad that they cancel all previous obligations. (In fact, Mr Sedley simply made some unlucky investments.) Mr Sedley is so bitter at the way that Mr Osborne has treated him that he forbids the marriage, too.

NOTES AND GLOSSARY:

Cornelia: a model of Roman womanhood, she lived in the second century BC

Potiphar's wife: she tempted Joseph to commit adultery with her. See the Bible, Genesis 39

Chapter 18: Who Played on the Piano Captain Dobbin Bought?

Dobbin goes to visit Amelia and her parents, who moved into lodgings owned by one of the employees in Mr Sedley's now bankrupt firm. When he sees Amelia, Dobbin is shocked at her appearance. He thinks that she will certainly die of a broken heart from losing George Osborne. Dobbin describes Amelia's plight to George, and prevails upon him to visit her.

NOTES AND GLOSSARY:

chasse à l'aigle: (*French*), an eagle hunt

Chapter 19: Miss Crawley as Nurse

Mrs Bute succeeds in installing herself as Miss Crawley's nurse. She confines Miss Crawley strictly to her room to prevent her from seeing Rawdon and Becky; if she saw them, she might forgive them.

NOTES AND GLOSSARY:

Hygeia: Greek goddess of health

Chapter 20: In Which Captain Dobbin Acts as the Messenger of Hymen

Dobbin has decided that Amelia and George should get married soon, for Amelia's sake and for his own. He loves Amelia himself, and the sooner the pain of her marriage is over, the less he will have suffered because of it. He sees Amelia's father, and has little trouble in persuading him to withdraw his ban on the marriage, particularly when he remarks that Mr Osborne will not like it.

NOTES AND GLOSSARY:

Hymen: Greek god of marriage

Esther: in the Bible, she becomes the Queen of King Ahasuerus of Persia (Esther 1-2)

three stars: she is an important stockholder in the company

Chapter 21: A Quarrel about an Heiress

George continues to visit Amelia. He tells her that a rich heiress, Amelia's old schoolmate Miss Swartz, has become a great favourite of his father and his sisters. One evening when Miss Swartz is visiting the Osbornes, she mentions Amelia, unaware that Mr Osborne has forbidden any mention of the Sedley family in his house. George's sisters make rude remarks about Amelia and her family. When George defends Amelia, his father overhears him and is enraged. Later that evening, George and his father quarrel. Mr Osborne tries to bully his son into marrying Miss Swartz for her money. When George refuses, Mr Osborne threatens to disinherit him and orders him out of the house.

NOTES AND GLOSSARY:

the Gazette: a newspaper which in time of war recorded the outcome of battles, exploits of bravery, and casualties

---

Chapter 22: A Marriage and Part of a Honeymoon

Prodded by Dobbin, George marries Amelia. Her brother Jos acts as the father of the bride, since Mr Sedley refuses to attend. Dobbin is the best man. No one else is present at the wedding except servants. The day is rainy and miserable.

The young couple go to the seaside resort of Brighton for their honeymoon, along with Jos. There they meet Rawdon and Becky. Miss Crawley's health began to deteriorate because of the confined life Mrs Bute had made her lead, and so Mrs Bute was forced to take her to Brighton (a sea resort south of London) for a change of scenery. When Becky and Rawdon learned this, they followed her to Brighton, hoping to see her and regain a place in her favour (and her will).

NOTES AND GLOSSARY:
'the morning I went out with Rocket': George 'went out' to fight a duel.

Chapter 23: Captain Dobbin Proceeds on his Canvas

Though Captain Dobbin is a shy and retiring man where his own affairs are concerned, he is active in attempting to help George and Amelia to win the forgiveness of Mr Osborne. He decides first to visit George's sisters and to gain their sympathy for the couple before he breaks the news of their marriage to Mr Osborne. Dobbin is successful in winning the young ladies' sympathy, particularly since the older daughter, Jane, wishes that Dobbin would marry her and accordingly has little to say against marriage in general. Unfortunately for Dobbin's plans, the two sisters immediately tell the news to Mr Fred Bullock, who is engaged to the younger of Mr Osborne's daughters. He reminds them both that if George is disinherited, they will inherit the very large sum of fifty thousand pounds. The girls' sympathy for their brother and his imprudent marriage fades.

NOTES AND GLOSSARY:
Dr Elliotson: a celebrated physician and hypnotist (1791-1868); Thackeray dedicated *Pendennis* to him

---

Chapter 24: In Which Mr Osborne Takes Down the Family Bible

Dobbin visits George's father at his office. Mr Osborne at first misinterprets Dobbin's arrival as a sign that George has given in and will agree to marry Miss Swartz. When he learns that George has married Amelia, he is furious. Dobbin leaves the office fearing the worst for his friend.

That evening, Mr Osborne refuses to speak to anyone. After dinner, he sits alone in his study. When a servant ventures in to place tea and a candle beside him, Osborne says nothing, but he locks the study door after the servant has left.

There follows one of the finest scenes in the novel, a scene which deserves the closest study. Thackeray gives a masterful picture of old Osborne's feelings about his son as he prepares to disinherit him. But all of his memories only strengthen his resolve. He takes down the family Bible and strikes George's name out of it. Then he burns his will, in which George figured prominently. The following morning, he goes to his office and meets his lawyer, who draws up a new will excluding George. Mr Osborne also directs the lawyer to write a letter to George, informing him that he is no longer a part of the family and that Mr Osborne will accept no communications of any kind from him. Mr Osborne has fulfilled his threat and disinherited his son for marrying Amelia, but the effort has shattered him.

NOTES AND GLOSSARY:

Abraham: In the Bible God commanded Abraham to sacrifice his son Isaac, but then relented (Genesis 22); Mr Osborne, however, will go through with his sacrifice of George

---

Chapter 25: In Which all the Principal Personages Think Fit to Leave Brighton

---

Dobbin hurries down to Brighton and delivers Mr Osborne's letter to George, who blames his misfortunes on Dobbin but calms down when Dobbin promises to help Amelia financially should the need arise. George's anxieties are prompted mainly by his own selfishness and his unwillingness to live on a small inheritance left him by his mother before she died. On the other hand, there is real cause for alarm, for Dobbin has learned during his stay in London that the regiment in which he and George serve will be fighting against Napoleon in a few weeks. It is thus possible that Amelia may soon be left a penniless widow. It now seems a pity that Dobbin hastened the marriage.

Amelia's short honeymoon is anything but pleasant, even before she learns the news that her husband will be going abroad. Rawdon Crawley wins a good deal of money from George. Worse still, Becky goes out of her way to fascinate George, who pays a great deal more attention to her than he does to his own wife. Amelia is no match for the brilliant, witty Becky; she feels inferior and excluded.

Rawdon and Becky are getting on very well, even though Miss Crawley is still in the hands of Mrs Bute. They have very little money, but they dress well enough to fool inn-keepers and tradesmen into thinking that they will pay their bills. Bailiffs, employed by those to whom Rawdon owes money, are waiting to arrest them in London for their debts, but word of their true financial condition has not yet reached Brighton.

Mrs Bute has become the virtual dictator of Miss Crawley and her household. But, as with so many characters in *Vanity Fair*, her plans bring unexpected results. She is actually too successful in imposing her will on Miss Crawley and her companions. They are afraid of her, but they also begin to hate her. Briggs finds Mrs Bute so unpleasant that she begins to relent toward Becky. Given a chance, Miss Crawley and her companions will rebel.

That chance comes when Mrs Bute's husband falls off a horse and becomes so ill that she is forced to return to nurse him. As soon as she leaves, Miss Crawley begins to do all the things that Mrs Bute forbade. She finds life much more pleasant this way and vows that Mrs Bute will never dominate her again.

But Mrs Bute was successful in poisoning Miss Crawley's mind against Becky and Rawdon. She found out as much as she could about Becky's disreputable family, and told all this and more to Miss Crawley. Thus when Becky tries to take advantage of Mrs Bute's departure to re-install herself and her husband in Miss Crawley's good graces, she fails.

NOTES AND GLOSSARY:
écarté:　　　　a card game.

Chapter 26: Between London and Chatham

Amelia's unhappy honeymoon draws to an early close, since George must rejoin his regiment in preparation for the coming campaign against the French. During their stay in London, George spends too much money and neglects Amelia. He goes to his father's lawyer to collect the small legacy left him by his mother. George expects to be treated as if he were a person of great importance. He does not realize that, now that he has been disinherited, the lawyer and his clerks only sneer at his attempts to act as if he were still a rich man.

George chooses not to accompany Amelia when she visits her parents. Amelia goes anyway. After she greets her parents, she sits for a while alone in her bedroom, thinking of how much she had looked forward to marrying George Osborne and how different the reality of being married is from her dreams.

NOTES AND GLOSSARY:
calipash or calipee: the best parts of the turtle.
'the allied sufferings': the allied sovereigns met in London to celebrate
their first victory over Napoleon in 1814.
pekin: civilian (Army slang).

Chapter 27: In Which Amelia Joins her Regiment

George and Amelia then go to Chatham, where the regiment is stationed.
There she is greeted by Dobbin, who has arrived earlier. She meets the
various officers and their wives, among them Major O'Dowd's wife,
Peggy, who is portrayed as a typical 'stage' Irishwoman, warm-hearted,
talkative, and proud of everything Irish.

NOTES AND GLOSSARY:
soirée: (*French*) evening party

Chapter 28: In Which Amelia Invades the Low Countries

The regiment then crosses the channel for Brussels, accompanied by
Amelia and Jos. Amelia is greatly admired by the soldiers and their
wives, and it becomes clearer than ever to the reader that Dobbin is
hopelessly in love with her. Amelia is unaware of this love. This is a
happy time for her. Away from Becky and the temptations of Brighton
or London, George treats Amelia as a newly-wed wife might expect to
be treated.

NOTES AND GLOSSARY:
'Pas si bête': (*French*) 'I'm not such a fool' as to have fought in
the battle of Waterloo
repayther: stage Irish for repeater, a kind of watch that strikes
the hours when a button is pressed
Catalani: Angelica Catalini (1780–1849), a famous soprano
singer

Chapter 29: Brussels

Amelia's happiness does not last long. Rawdon Crawley arrives in
Brussels with Becky, who succeeds in fascinating nearly all the officers
gathered in Brussels. Becky goes out of her way to attract George, even
though this makes Amelia miserable. She has always resented Amelia
for coming from a prosperous family, and she has a score to settle with

George for preventing her marriage with Jos. By attracting George to herself, she provides another victim for her husband to cheat at the gaming table.

George's infatuation reaches its peak at a ball held, as it turns out, on the eve of battle against Napoleon. He ignores Amelia all night; at the end of the evening, he slips a note to Becky into a bouquet which he gives her. Amelia sees George give Becky the bouquet; whether she sees the letter is left unclear. The bouquet is enough. She asks Dobbin to take her home. He does so, after which he returns to the ball. Dobbin has just learned that Napoleon is already approaching Brussels. His regiment will be fighting in a few hours. When George learns this sobering news, he is filled with remorse for the way he has treated Amelia. He returns to their hotel and says goodbye to her tenderly before leaving for the battle.

NOTES AND GLOSSARY:

'the Juke':	Arthur Wellesley, Duke of Wellington (1769–1852), commander-in-chief of the allied forces opposing Napoleon at Waterloo
Darius:	Darius the Great, King of Persia (521–484 BC), raised a huge army to invade Greece; he was defeated

Chapter 30: 'The Girl I Left Behind Me'

Amelia is beside herself with fear for George as he leaves for battle. Peggy O'Dowd, an experienced campaigner, is just as concerned for her husband's safety, but she takes his departure more stoically. Becky for her part seems utterly indifferent about Rawdon's safety, though she hides this fact from him. Rawdon leaves three horses and as much other property as he can spare with Becky, since he wants her to have something to live on if anything happens to him.

NOTES AND GLOSSARY:

Manton:	this and the other names Rawdon mentions refer to shops in London

Chapter 31: In Which Jos Sedley Takes Care of his Sister

After the men have gone, Becky visits a bank to cash a draft which George Osborne had given Rawdon to pay off gambling debts. Then she visits Amelia. But Amelia is not quite so naive as she was when the novel opened. She refuses to take Becky's hand. She asks angrily why

Becky has tried to ruin her happiness by luring away George. Even Becky is touched by her intense fear that something will happen to George during the battle. Since Amelia refuses to have anything to do with her, Becky leaves. When she happens upon Peggy O'Dowd, however, she mentions that Amelia is unwell and needs someone to look after her, and Peggy is good enough to visit Amelia and take care of her.

NOTES AND GLOSSARY:

'C'est le feu!':   (*French*) 'It's the cannons!'

Chapter 32: In Which Jos Takes Flight, and the War is Brought to a Close

---

The incidents in Brussels during the battle of Waterloo are not all serious. Comedy is provided by Amelia's brother Jos, who has been travelling with George's regiment. Early in the novel Thackeray told us that Jos was a coward during the only tiger hunt which he attended in India; now Jos has a chance to prove it. The battle lasts several days. As it progresses, reports come in that the English are losing badly. Jos at first disbelieves these reports, but his nerve breaks before too long and he panics. He had grown an enormous, military-style moustache. Now he cuts it off, since he hears a rumour that the French are killing all their military prisoners.

Jos decides to run away from Brussels. Unfortunately, there are no horses, since civilians who panicked earlier have already taken them all. This puts Becky in a strong position, for she still has the horses which Rawdon left for her. Becky first amuses herself by taking revenge on an English noblewoman, Lady Bareacres, who had been rude to her during her stay in Brussels. She forces Lady Bareacres to beg for the horses in person, but refuses to sell them to her anyway. Ultimately she sells them, at a tremendously high price, to Jos, who is so terrified of the French that he leaves without Amelia when she refuses to go anywhere until she knows what has happened to her husband. As it turns out, the English win the battle, so that Jos has wasted his money on the horses. Not long afterwards, Jos returns to India, where he brags about his courageous exploits at the battle of Waterloo.

Amelia's fears for George prove prophetic. He survives the initial days of fighting, but is killed during the climax of the battle of Waterloo.

NOTES AND GLOSSARY:

'Pas de cheveaux': (*French*) 'There are no more horses!'
'Coupez-moi, vite': the French can mean either 'cut my hair' (or whiskers) or 'cut me' (hence 'cut my throat')

Chapter 33: In Which Miss Crawley's Relations are Very Anxious about her

The scene now changes to England and the fortunes of Miss Crawley. Now that Mrs Bute and Rawdon have eliminated themselves from being potential heirs, who will inherit her money? Rawdon's older brother, Pitt Crawley, steps in to fill the gap. He had never been a favourite with Miss Crawley. Until now in the novel, he has appeared to be rather a priggish man, dedicated to a humourless style of religion. Now he reveals other qualities. As the narrator reminds us, he was once in the diplomatic service, and he uses his diplomatic skill to win Miss Crawley's favour. Unlike Mrs Bute, he does not try to run Miss Crawley's life: in fact, he prevents his future mother-in-law, Lady Southdown, from trying to do so. And unlike Rawdon, he is about to form an eminently respectable marriage, with Lady Jane Sheepshanks, a kind, gentle woman who despite the absurd name Thackeray gives her turns out to be perhaps the most admirable character in the entire novel.

NOTES AND GLOSSARY:
C.B.:   Companion of the Bath, a military honour Rawdon has received for bravery in battle.
Machiavellian: a subtle intriguer, as the Florentine political theorist Niccolo Machiavelli (1469–1527) was said to be

Chapter 34: James Crawley's Pipe is Put Out

At one point, Pitt's plans seem on the verge of being upset. Mrs Bute sends her son James to visit Miss Crawley, in a last desperate attempt to regain her favour. Unfortunately for Mrs Bute, James has low tastes. Pitt pretends to be James's friend, and encourages him to act just as he likes while he lives with Miss Crawley. The boy is stupid enough to do so. He drinks too much, acts rudely, and the final straw comes when he smokes in his bedroom. Miss Crawley abhors the smell of tobacco, which filters throughout the house. She sends him packing the next morning. Pitt's success is assured when Miss Crawley becomes fond of Lady Jane. Word comes from Paris, where Becky and Rawdon have moved after Waterloo, that Becky has had a son. Any chance that Miss Crawley will forgive the pair now vanishes. Becky's child is too dramatic a reminder of the disgraceful marriage Rawdon has made with the daughter of a French opera dancer. Miss Crawley demands that Pitt and Lady Jane marry at once, and promises to leave them all her money. After their marriage, they live with her until she dies a short time later.

NOTES AND GLOSSARY:

Mr Fox: Charles James Fox (1749–1806), a Whig statesman who took a conciliatory stance toward France during the Napoleonic wars and hence was a favourite with Miss Crawley

'In vino veritas': (*Latin*) 'Wine makes people speak the truth'

'Mars, Bacchus, Apollo virorum': a phrase from James's Latin grammar book

'Nunc vino ... aequor': 'Now let us chase away care with wine; tomorrow we set out again over the sea.' The words appear in an Ode (I, vii) by the Roman poet Horace (who lived from 65 BC to 8 BC)

Chapter 35: Widow and Mother

When Mr Osborne learns of George's death, he erects a monument to his memory in the church which the Osborne family attend in London. He also visits the battlefield where George fought and died, as well as his grave. During this trip he happens to see Amelia and Dobbin, but when Dobbin tells him that Amelia is destitute, old Osborne refuses to help her. He hates Amelia, because she was the reason why George disobeyed him and died unreconciled to him.

Dobbin himself does his best to take care of the young widow, who still does not realise that he loves her. He sees to it that she arrives safely back at her parents' house in London, where she has a child some months later. She names him George, after his father, and centres all her affection on him.

NOTES AND GLOSSARY:

Pax in bello: (*Latin*) 'Peace in war'; the motto is grimly appropriate to George, who has found in war the peace of death

Dulce et decorum ... mori: (*Latin*) 'It is a sweet and appropriate thing to die for your country' (Horace, Odes III, ii)

Chapter 36: How to Live Well on Nothing A-Year

Becky and Rawdon have been living in Paris in their usual style. They manage to live well without an income, by convincing their creditors that they will eventually pay bills, although they have neither the intention of paying them nor the money to pay them. Becky enjoys their social life, but she realises that there is no future for them abroad. She convinces Rawdon that he should sell his place in the army. Then she settles their debts in England by paying a small portion of what they actually owe: at this point, their creditors are happy to get anything at all.

NOTES AND GLOSSARY:
Mrs Grundy: proverbial guardian of propriety

Chapter 37: The Subject Continued

Becky and Rawdon return to London. They move into a house rented to them by an old Crawley family servant who had used his earnings to become independent. Once again they begin to live on credit. Becky runs into the late Miss Crawley's companion Briggs, and engages her as her own companion. Becky needs to have a female companion around the house to preserve her respectability, for she has taken to entertaining all sorts of men. These men, she hopes, will make her fortune. The most powerful of them is the notorious nobleman, Lord Steyne.

Leading the sort of life she does, Becky has little interest in her young son, the child whose birth so angered Miss Crawley. Rawdon adores the child, however, and takes him on frequent walks. On one of these excursions, young Rawdon and his father meet young George Osborne and his grandfather.

NOTES AND GLOSSARY:
Corydon: like Meliboeus, the name of a shepherd who figures
                     in pastoral poetry celebrating the simple virtues of
                     country life, such as playing the pipe; an ironic
                     reference to Rawdon and his gambling
a knight of the Order: Steyne is in fact a Knight of the Golden Fleece,
                     the highest order of Spain; also, he has 'sheared'
                     opponents at cards (won all their money), and
                     indeed won his title by doing so

Chapter 38: A Family in a Very Small Way

Dobbin has all the while been doing what he can for George and his mother, sending them financial support and presents of various kinds from his army post in India, where he is now a Major. All of the men who come into contact with Amelia are touched and charmed by her, but she lives only for her son and for the memory of her dead husband. Her mother is angry at this devotion. She realises that Dobbin is in love with Amelia, and wishes that Amelia would marry him. Nothing seems farther from Amelia's thoughts. However, when the Dobbin sisters (who sometimes visit her, obviously at the request of their brother) tell Amelia that there is a rumour that Dobbin is going to marry Peggy O'Dowd's sister, Glorvina, Amelia seems upset by the news.

NOTES AND GLOSSARY:

parliament: a kind of gingerbread

Jack Ketch: a brutal seventeenth-century executioner; the name came to be used to refer to hangmen in general

Chapter 39: A Cynical Chapter

After Becky refused his offer of marriage, Sir Pitt Crawley began to live in a scandalous, immoral manner. He carried on with the daughter of his butler Horrocks, giving her gifts and laughing at her absurd attempts to play the gentlewoman. The ancestral home was allowed to decay. None of Sir Pitt's former friends would associate with him.

Sir Pitt's sense of humour finally proves his undoing. One day, Miss Horrocks tries to play the piano and sing. Her attempts amuse Sir Pitt, who laughs uproariously and drinks even more than usual. That night, he suffers a paralytic stroke. He never recovers and dies soon afterwards. After his stroke, his relatives send Miss Horrocks away scornfully.

NOTES AND GLOSSARY:

Bulbul: an eastern songbird; hence a poet

calash: a woman's bonnet; used to refer to Mrs Bute

Chapter 40: In Which Becky is Recognised by the Family

Old Sir Pitt's title of Baronet and property pass to Pitt, who arrives with his wife Lady Jane and his mother-in-law Lady Southdown. Lady Southdown had dominated Pitt and his wife ever since their marriage, but now that he is a Baronet and a land-owner, Pitt decides to stand for this no longer. When Lady Southdown threatens to leave if the family invites Becky to old Sir Pitt's funeral, Pitt invites her anyway. He knows that the Countess will back down, since leaving Queen's Crawley would be inconvenient for her at the moment. Lady Southdown does indeed stay for the funeral, and Pitt becomes the undisputed head of the family.

NOTES AND GLOSSARY:

Silenus: a demi-god, foster father of Bacchus, usually represented as a fat, drunken old man

Chapter 41: In Which Becky Revisits the Halls of her Ancestors

Becky is delighted with the invitation to Queen's Crawley, for it seems a step toward gaining the respectability and financial independence she has always wanted. When she arrives at Queen's Crawley, she makes it her business to ingratiate herself with everyone there. As usual, she succeeds, even with Lady Southdown herself.

NOTES AND GLOSSARY:

Consols: government securities

Chapter 42: Which Treats of the Osborne Family

In this chapter, Thackeray gives a brilliant picture of the gloomy life Mr Osborne has been leading since his son's death. One of his daughters has married, and he lives alone in his mansion, waited on by his other child, Miss Jane Osborne, who is terrified of him and leads a miserable existence.

One day Miss Osborne happens to meet Amelia's son George, who is visiting the Dobbins when she calls on them. That evening, she tells Mr Osborne that she has seen his grandson, who resembles his father very much. Osborne says nothing, but the emotion which he shows at hearing about his grandson suggests that he may weaken in his resolve never to see either Amelia or her son.

NOTES AND GLOSSARY:

R.A.: a member of the Royal Academy, a prestigious society of artists

Chapter 43: In Which the Reader Has to Double the Cape

Major Dobbin has in the meantime continued to serve in the army in India. The report that he and Glorvina O'Dowd were to be married turns out to be false. She has been pursuing him, but he is not interested in anyone but Amelia. This interest is so strong that when he receives a letter from his sister, stating that Amelia is soon to be married, Dobbin immediately requests leave from the army and starts at once on the long trip back to England. Perhaps he can stop the marriage; at least he wants to know about it at first hand.

NOTES AND GLOSSARY:

zenanas: the women's apartments in Indian households

Lassata nondum . . .: Latin quotation from the Roman satirist Juvenal (*c.* 60–130). This describes the Empress Messalina leaving a brothel—'wearied but not yet sated, she withdrew'—and Thackeray is using it somewhat ironically here of Lady O'Dowd

Desdemona: heroine of Shakespeare's *Othello*; Othello won her love by recounting the dangers and adventures he had undergone

---

Chapter 44: A Round-About Chapter between London and Hampshire

Back in London, Becky continues her struggle for social position and fortune. Her intimacy with Lord Steyne increases. The servants and her landlord are convinced that she has become Lord Steyne's mistress, though the narrator tells us that she is probably innocent.

NOTES AND GLOSSARY:

Vehmgericht: (*German*) a medieval German tribunal. It often met in subterranean vaults; hence it provides an appropriate metaphor for the servants' comments on their masters upstairs

---

Chapter 45: Between Hampshire and London

Becky makes it her business to ingratiate herself with Pitt Crawley. She takes charge of refurbishing his London mansion and encourages him to seek a career in Parliament, which he does by entertaining his neighbours on a lavish scale. He also drops his strict religious views, at which Lady Southdown departs in disgust. Pitt becomes increasingly dissatisfied with his own wife and fond of Becky.

One male who does not interest Becky at all is her own son, young Rawdon. She dislikes having him around the house; perhaps she fears that he will see her doing something improper and tell Rawdon about it. Rawdon tries to love his mother. One day he sneaks downstairs to listen to her sing to Lord Steyne. Becky opens the door to the living room and discovers her son standing there, and she slaps him in the face. The boy never forgives her. When the family visit Pitt at Queen's

Crawley, young Rawdon has a wonderful time, but Lady Jane is pained to learn that Rawdon never eats with his mother and indeed that his mother never kisses him, except to make a good impression in public. Lady Jane begins to suspect Becky. Her suspicions become hidden dislike when she realises that her own husband, Pitt, has become infatuated with Becky. For her part, Becky despises Lady Jane for her love of children and domestic life.

NOTES AND GLOSSARY:
cortège: (*French*) procession

Chapter 46: Struggles and Trials

Becky's fortunes seem to be on the rise. For Amelia and her family, things are different. Mr Sedley tries to regain his fortune in various ways, all of which fail. The family begins to go into debt. Worst of all, Mr Sedley tells them that the allowance which Jos had been sending from India to support them is no longer arriving.

Mr Osborne offers to adopt George and give Amelia in return for custody of the boy a small living allowance for her and her parents. Amelia will only be able to see her son from time to time in her own home, for Mr Osborne still refuses to see her. Amelia does not agree to these terms when the offer is made, but her family's worsening financial situation poses her with a cruel dilemma. If only she could bear to be separated from young George, she could assure him, and her own mother and father as well, of a comfortable life.

NOTES AND GLOSSARY:
in Eutropius: in a lower form at school
'My name is Norval': a speech often recited as a schoolboy exercise; it
                         is from *Douglas*, by John Home (1722–1808)

Chapter 47: Gaunt House

In Chapters 47–9, Thackeray gives a brilliant if depressing picture of Lord Steyne and his family, designed to show that even a great nobleman may not be so fortunate as he appears to be. Lord Steyne has long since ceased to love his wife. He and his older son hate each other, since the son wishes the father were dead so that he could inherit his position and wealth. What is more, there is a taint of madness in the family. Steyne's younger son married, had children, and was beginning a promising diplomatic career when he suddenly became insane and had to be confined. Lord Steyne believes that at any moment the same thing could happen to him.

NOTES AND GLOSSARY:
the Prince and Perdita: George IV and one of his mistresses
Oxford against St Acheul: colleges for clergy of the Church of England and the Catholic Church, respectively

---

Chapter 48: In Which the Reader is Introduced into the Very Best of Company

Becky continues to rise socially. Pitt Crawley presents her at court, where she kisses the King's hand. This act in itself makes her a respectable woman in the eyes of polite society.

NOTES AND GLOSSARY:
the First Gentleman in Europe: George IV was so considered because of his elegant dress and manners. Thackeray held him in contempt: his remark that as a child he had seen 'George the Good' is ironic
Maintenon: The Marquise de Maintenon (1635–1719) was one of King Louis XIV of France's mistresses, and afterwards became his wife. The Marquise de Pompadour (1721–64) was a mistress of Louis XV. Becky has designs on George IV
Regan and Goneril: the two evil daughters in Shakespeare's *King Lear*

Chapter 49: In Which We Enjoy Three Courses and a Dessert

The Marquis of Steyne bullies his wife and daughters-in-law into inviting Becky and Rawdon to a dinner party. The women are rude to her, until Lady Steyne has pity on her and invites her to sing for them. But the men, as usual, are enchanted. For the time being at least, Becky has arrived at the social heights she has always desired to reach. Her other goal, wealth, continues to elude her.

NOTES AND GLOSSARY:
Young Marlow: a young man who is exceedingly bashful with respectable, upper-class women, including the heroine Miss Hardcastle, in the play *She Stoops to Conquer* by Oliver Goldsmith (1730–74)

Chapter 50: Contains a Vulgar Incident

Amelia's family sinks slowly but surely deeper into debt, and life becomes harsh. Amelia tries to remedy matters by writing to Jos, reminding him that he has forgotten to send them their allowance. When she tells her father what she has done, she learns the truth. Jos has continued to send the allowance all along, but instead of going to the family, it has been used to pay off a loan which Mr Sedley raised for one of his unsuccessful business ventures. There is only one way left to avoid ruin. Amelia agrees to send her son George to live with the Osbornes. Doing so wracks her with grief. Young George, on the other hand, is delighted at the prospect of living in a rich house and going to an exclusive school.

NOTES AND GLOSSARY:

Lady Jane Grey: the victim of a plot which sought to make her Queen of England, instead of Mary I; she was beheaded in 1553

Chapter 51: In Which a Charade is Acted which May or May not Puzzle the Reader

In this section of the novel, Becky's social success comes to an abrupt, dramatic end. Thackeray presents her sudden downfall with great skill. First he lets us see Becky at the height of her powers, successful and admired by the highest London society and even by the King himself. A party at Lord Steyne's is the scene of Becky's triumph, where an elaborate set of charades, in which the actors act out words which the audience tries to guess, provides the perfect setting for her powers as an actress.

After the charades are over, Becky takes the family carriage home. Rawdon does not join her. Lord Steyne's man of business, Mr Wenham, has suggested that he and Rawdon walk home together and smoke a cigar on the way. But almost immediately after they leave Lord Steyne's mansion, Rawdon finds himself surrounded by bailiffs, who arrest him for one of his many debts. Rawdon is driven away to a 'sponging-house', a sort of private debtors' prison, where he will be given a short time to come up with the money he owes before more extreme proceedings are taken against him.

NOTES AND GLOSSARY:

Sir Walter Scott: great Scottish novelist and poet (1771–1832)

the Great Pitt:	William Pitt (1759–1806) was a British statesman of the time, as were Henry Dundas (1742–1811) and Henry Addington (1757–1844). Lady Hester was Pitt's niece
Brian de Bois Guilbert:	the villain of Scott's novel *Ivanhoe*, who brings back a black servant to England from the Holy Land
Clytemnestra:	wife of Agamemnon, she murdered him to avenge his sacrifice of their daughter Iphigenia. Aegisthus was her lover

---

Chapter 52: In Which Lord Steyne Shows Himself in a Most Amiable Light

---

Thackeray now leaves us in uncertainty about Rawdon's situation. He breaks his narration to tell us about various acts of seeming kindness which Lord Steyne has recently shown toward Rawdon's family. Steyne found a place for young Rawdon at a private school where the boy's education costs his parents nothing. The nobleman next turned his attention to Becky's companion Miss Briggs (who, as the reader will recall, was hired to preserve Becky's reputation by acting as her companion). Becky had earlier obtained £1200 from Steyne to repay the money she borrowed from Briggs soon after hiring her. Now Steyne discovered that Becky had used his money for other purposes. Briggs received none of it; in fact, Becky only owed Briggs £600 in the first place. Steyne was not angry at being tricked, but instead amused at the skill with which Becky had deceived him. He decided to take care of Briggs by offering her the job of housekeeper at one of his country homes.

At this point, Rawdon began to be suspicious. He thought that Steyne's seeming generosity might simply be an attempt to get rid of the two people who could prevent the nobleman from seeing Becky alone. Rawdon began to accompany Becky everywhere and to stay at home at night, though it was hard for him to believe that she intended to betray him.

This narrative digression concerning Lord Steyne's favours to the Crawley family puts us as readers in the position in which Rawdon finds himself when he is arrested—full of suspicions (has Steyne used Wenham to set Rawdon up for the arrest?) but sure of nothing.

NOTES AND GLOSSARY:

Astley's:	a London circus

Chapter 53: A Rescue and a Catastrophe

When Rawdon arrives at the sponging-house, he waits until morning before trying to contact Becky, since he does not want to disturb her sleep. Then he writes her a letter, asking her to send him £100 to settle the debt. Her reply takes much longer than it should to arrive. When it finally comes, it infuriates Rawdon. Becky makes some unconvincing excuses and sends nothing. He will have to stay in the jail for another night.

Rawdon immediately writes a letter to Pitt and Lady Jane, asking their help. Pitt is not home, but Lady Jane brings the money and liberates Rawdon. It is night by now. When Rawdon returns home, he discovers Becky alone with Lord Steyne. Steyne is furious at being disturbed. He had assumed all along that Rawdon knew that Becky was receiving large sums of money from him. In Steyne's eyes, Rawdon has sold Becky to him. Steyne tells Rawdon as much, but he has been mistaken. Rawdon slaps the Marquis twice, knocking him to the floor. He strips Becky of the jewels which Steyne had given her and demands to know whether or not Steyne had given her money also. Becky tries to lie, but Rawdon rips through all of her belongings until he finds a £1000 note, part of the money Becky had received from Steyne earlier, supposedly to pay back Briggs. Rawdon then leaves. Becky swears that she is innocent (that is, that she has not had sexual relations with Steyne). But she knows that Rawdon will never come back.

NOTES AND GLOSSARY:
placens uxor: (*Latin*) 'Dear wife' (Horace, Odes II, xiv)

Chapter 54: Sunday after the Battle

After he leaves Becky, Rawdon goes to see his brother Pitt. He believes that a duel is inevitable between himself and Lord Steyne. If Rawdon is killed, someone will have to look after young Rawdon, since Becky never liked him and has anyway forfeited any right to him in Rawdon's eyes. Pitt agrees to take care of the boy if anything happens to his father.

Rawdon then visits an old army friend named Macmurdo, whom he asks to be his second in the duel with Lord Steyne. According to the code of honour, the only possible response Steyne could make to being physically assaulted would be to duel with Rawdon. But Steyne decides to avoid the duel anyway. Instead, he sends his man of business Wenham to smooth things over. Wenham tells Rawdon that he is mistaken in his suspicions about Lord Steyne and Becky. He swears that he and his wife had been invited to dinner with Becky on the night when Rawdon found her alone with Steyne, but at the last minute they could not attend. Thus Becky did not intend to be alone with the Marquis. This explanation seems extremely far-fetched, especially since Wenham cannot find the letter of invitation he pretends to have received from Becky. Rawdon wants to proceed with the duel anyway, but his army friend persuades him not to do so. If Lord Steyne is willing to swallow the gross affront of having been struck by Rawdon, that is the end of the matter. Rawdon must content himself with returning Steyne's £1000 note.

Another reason why Macmurdo wants Rawdon to give up the idea of pursuing the quarrel is announced in the morning newspaper. Lord Steyne has obtained for Rawdon the post of governor of one of the islands in the British Empire. According to Macmurdo, Rawdon should accept the post and forget about anything Steyne may have done to him. (It seems likely that Steyne got the job for Rawdon to put him out of the way—as Briggs and young Rawdon have already been—since the climate of the island is very unhealthy, and it is hard to imagine Becky's staying there for very long, if indeed she was willing to accompany Rawdon there in the first place.) Rawdon unwillingly accepts the appointment so that he can support his son. He also thinks that Steyne, who got him the job before their quarrel over Becky, will be furious to have benefited a man who struck him down.

NOTES AND GLOSSARY:
triste: (*French*) sad

Chapter 55: In Which the Same Subject is Pursued

Meanwhile Becky finds that the servants are aware of what has happened. They had assumed that Steyne would pay her debts. Now her landlords will be ruined themselves, since they have gone into debt to provide food for the Crawleys' dinners. When they see her, they are understandably rude to her. In a few hours, Becky has fallen from the apex of society to this! One last chance remains. She visits Pitt and uses all her charm to convince him that she is innocent. He promises to help her, but when Lady Jane finds Pitt and Becky together, she shows surprising firmness. Either Becky leaves the house, Lady Jane tells Pitt, or she will herself. Becky leaves, and Pitt is unable to persuade Rawdon to forgive her. Pitt keeps his promise to take care of young Rawdon, who continues at school and becomes a kind of son to Pitt and Lady Jane. Rawdon travels to his island and vows never to see Becky again.

NOTES AND GLOSSARY
affreusement volé: (French) 'scandalously cheated'

Chapter 56: Georgy is Made a Gentleman

Young George Osborne has meanwhile gained complete ascendency over everyone involved in the Osborne household. Even his grandfather, utterly tyrannical in his dealings with everyone else, humours the boy.

Amelia must content herself with infrequent visits from George. Her mother dies, and she is left alone with her father, whose feeble health requires constant attention.

One day when George is at school, two gentlemen arrive to see him. They are Dobbin and Jos Sedley.

NOTES AND GLOSSARY
aristos, optimus, très bien: 'excellent' in Greek, Latin, and French, respectively

---

Chapter 57: Eothen

Jos's health had begun to be affected by the Indian climate. He decided to return to England, and met Dobbin on the way. Dobbin had fallen extremely ill on his way back to England, but when Jos assured him that the rumour about Amelia's impending marriage was false, Dobbin quickly recovered. During their voyage together, Dobbin convinced Jos that he should set up house in London. Amelia could act as the lady of the house, and his parents could live with them.

NOTES AND GLOSSARY
Eothen: title of an account of his eastern travels by A.W. Kinglake (1809–91). The reference is to Dobbin, also an eastern traveller

---

Chapter 58: Our Old Friend the Major

As soon as he arrives in England, Dobbin hurries to London, leaving Jos behind at Southampton. When he arrives in London, Dobbin goes immediately to visit Amelia. He is delighted to learn at first-hand that she is not married.

NOTES AND GLOSSARY:
chillum: water-pipe
grandes eaux: (*French*) 'fountains'; that is, she began to cry.

Chapter 59: The Old Piano

Dobbin tells Amelia that he loves her. She replies that she still considers herself bound to the dead George Osborne, though she values Dobbin's friendship. For the moment, at least, Dobbin must be content with this.

When Jos arrives in London, he buys a house. Amelia and her father move in with him. Her fortunes are on the rise.

NOTES AND GLOSSARY:

Persicos apparatus: (*Latin*) Persian luxury (Horace, Odes, I, xxxviii)

Chapter 60: Returns to the Genteel World

Now that Amelia has entered the genteel world again and her wealthy brother Jos is no longer ignoring the family, old Mr Osborne begins to look more favourably on the Sedleys. He adores little George, and hopes that Jos will leave his estate to George when he dies.

NOTES AND GLOSSARY:

ami de la maison: (*French*) friend of the family

mutato nomine: (*Latin*) if you change the name of the profession

Chapter 61: In Which Two Lights are Put Out

When old Mr Sedley dies, the way toward a reconciliation between Amelia and Mr Osborne is smoothed. He invites Jos and Dobbin to dinner, and seems ready to forgive Amelia for having married his son. He changes his will, leaving half of his property to George and a generous annuity to Amelia. But before he has a chance to meet Amelia for the first time since her marriage, he dies.

Meanwhile, acquaintances who paid no attention at all to Amelia when she was poor now cluster around her. These women are all interested in improving and 'forming' Amelia. The life of this social circle is dreary, and Jos, Amelia, Dobbin, and George decide to visit Europe.

NOTES AND GLOSSARY:

wears a front: wears false curls on her forehead to hide her age.
'Some of the ladies were very blue': they were or affected to be highly educated

Chapter 62: Am Rhein

Amelia and her friends travel through Germany until they arrive at the principality of Pumpernickel (Thackeray's name for Weimar). There they take up quarters for the Autumn, visiting the opera, calling on the local nobility, and generally enjoying themselves.

NOTES AND GLOSSARY:
'His Transparency': a literal translation of a German title like His
Excellency, which obviously amuses Thackeray

Chapter 63: In Which We Meet an Old Acquaintance

One evening when Amelia, Jos, and Dobbin are away, young George persuades the family servant to take him to the casino. There he meets a short, sandy-haired woman who, like several other women there, is wearing a mask. She asks him to bet for her at the roulette table, for she wants to take advantage of his beginner's luck. She wins, but Dobbin and Jos come in immediately afterwards. Dobbin leads George away and tells him never to gamble again, but Jos dawdles there by the roulette table. The short woman engages Jos in conversation, and finally reveals that she is Becky. She complains of her sufferings since Rawdon left her, and asks Jos to visit her at her hotel.

NOTES AND GLOSSARY:
'Monsieur n'est pas joueur?': (*French*) 'You are not a gambler?'
'Laissez-moi tranquille...': (*French*) 'Leave me alone; one has to
relax sometimes. I'm not your servant anyway'

Chapter 64: A Vagabond Chapter

Becky has had her troubles since the evening when Rawdon discovered her alone with Lord Steyne. Respectable society in England disowned her. Pitt Crawley's opinion of her was poisoned by Lord Steyne's man Wenham, who told Pitt damaging things about her. Lady Jane also continued to refuse to have anything to do with her. Rawdon allowed her three hundred pounds a year, on condition that she would never bother him.

Shut out of society in England, Becky went to the Continent, but whenever she gathered a circle of friends in one of the English émigré communities there, someone who had known her in England would arrive, blacken her character, and she would have to move on.

Her travels led her to Rome, where she was able to get an invitation to an important party. At dinner she looked up at the head table, and saw—Lord Steyne. He also saw her. Would he forgive her, perhaps even take her up as his mistress, Becky wondered? On the following day, one of Steyne's attendants brought the answer. He warned Becky that she would be killed if she stayed in Rome. Steyne had never forgiven her; indeed, part of her difficulty in finding a place in respectable society had been caused by his agents.

Becky had already developed a passion for gambling and a liking for unconventional society. After her experiences in Rome, those tastes increased. Finally her travels led her to Pumpernickel and thus to Amelia, Jos and Dobbin.

NOTES AND GLOSSARY:

Doctors' Commons: the law court that handled divorces

Nym and Pistol: disreputable soldiers who appear in Shakespeare's *Henry V*

Banquo: a character in Shakespeare's *Macbeth*. Macbeth arranges for his murder, but the ghost of Banquo appears at a subsequent banquet, much to Macbeth's horror

---

Chapter 65: Full of Business and Pleasure

The day after he meets Becky at the Casino, Jos dresses himself with more than usual care and goes to visit her at her hotel. Becky quickly enchants him, persuading him that it is Rawdon who is guilty for their separation and her present mode of life. Jos returns home, full of plans for rescuing Becky. Amelia is won over to Becky's side when Jos recounts one of the lies which Becky invented to secure his sympathy. Becky had said that her son, young Rawdon, had been torn from her arms, and that she is broken-hearted at having been separated from him (whereas the truth is that she never liked the boy). Amelia remembers her own pain at giving up her son to the Osbornes. Her sympathy is awakened, and she forgets the ways in which Becky mistreated her in the past.

NOTES AND GLOSSARY:

sournois: (*French*) cunning

'Quarterfang tooce!': the spelling is meant to represent the student saying Becky's room number in French but with a German accent

Chapter 66: *Amantium Irae*

Dobbin is opposed to the plan which Jos and Amelia have formed of bringing Becky to live with them. An argument ensues. Dobbin, angry at the way in which Amelia ignores his judgement and disturbed at the effect which Becky may have on the family, reminds Amelia that Becky was not always a very good friend to her. He is referring, of course, to the way in which Becky flirted with George Osborne in the days after George and Amelia were married.

Things between Dobbin and Amelia have come to a crisis. That night, she realises that she will have to choose between the memory of her dead husband and Dobbin, but she cannot bring herself to marry him. The next day she tells Dobbin that she will never forgive him for his reference to George's flirtations with Becky; furthermore, Becky is going to become part of the Sedley establishment, whether he likes it or not.

One of the greatest scenes in nineteenth-century fiction follows. Amelia is in some respects a paragon. She is selflessly devoted to her child and faithful to the memory of her husband. Dobbin now tells this seeming image of female perfection that she is not worthy of him. Her love extends only to her own dreams, not to reality. His own love has been worn out by the long process of trying to win her and going unrewarded. He is now free of the chain that has bound him to her for so long. Such an attack on Amelia is a remarkable challenge to a certain kind of sentimental fiction popular in Thackeray's day; it weighs and finds wanting a heavily entrenched vision of feminine virtue.

Dobbin leaves. Amelia has remained faithful to the memory of George, but she is miserable.

NOTES AND GLOSSARY:
Amantium irae: (*Latin*) the anger of lovers
fumum and *strepitus:* (*Latin*) smoke and noise (Horace, Odes III, xxix)
saufen and *singen:* (*German*) drinking and singing
manchen Sturm erlebt: (German) lasted through many storms

Chapter 67: Which Contains Births, Marriages, and Deaths

Becky continues to live with Jos and Amelia. She bends all of her efforts toward winning the favour of the household; as usual, she succeeds. She discovers that to please Amelia, all she needs to do is to talk about what a fine man Dobbin is. Becky gets around Jos in a different way. The reader will recall that in the early part of the novel, Becky and

Rawdon had happened upon the sale of old Mr Sedley's belongings, where they amused themselves by buying a picture of Jos riding on an elephant. Becky still possesses the picture. She tells Jos that she has saved it out of love for him, and her conquest of the portly Anglo-Indian is complete.

With the coming of summer, the little society at Pumpernickel disperses. Jos, his sister, and Becky go to the resort of Ostend, a place which Becky had frequented in her more disreputable days. Two former gentlemen friends of hers begin to make advances toward Amelia, which alarm her and annoy Becky. Amelia has missed Dobbin ever since he left her; now her uncomfortable situation is too much for her. Without telling anyone, she sends him a letter.

Becky decides the very same day that it is time to put a stop to Amelia's persecution by the two men. All along, Becky has kept the letter which George Osborne put in her bouquet at the ball on the eve of the battle of Waterloo. She shows the note to Amelia as proof that George was not worth all the devotion Amelia has shown his memory. Amelia reads the letter, only to learn that George had actually asked Becky to run off with him. Amelia is sad to see her idol shattered, but also relieved: now she can marry Dobbin without guilt or regret.

Dobbin returns, and he and Amelia are married. They rent a house near Queen's Crawley, to which Pitt and Lady Jane had retired after the failure of Pitt's political career. Pitt had controlled two parliamentary seats, but the Reform Act of 1832 abolished the seats and with them his political influence. Pitt died not long after; since Pitt's son and Rawdon had also died in the meantime, young Rawdon succeeded to his uncle's title and property.

Jos meanwhile remained on the Continent; he travelled with Becky. Amelia learns that he has insured his life for a large sum. Alarmed, she prevails upon Dobbin to visit Jos on the Continent and make sure that he is all right. Dobbin finds Jos infirm. He wants to break away from Becky but is afraid to do so, and Dobbin is forced to return to England without him. A few months later he is dead. Circumstances suggest that he might have been murdered by Becky, but there is no proof of this. It appears that she has possessed herself of Jos's fortune through devious means, since all he leaves behind are his insurance policy and shares in worthless and probably fictitious companies. Becky returns to England seemingly a well-to-do woman. She regains something of a good reputation by appearing regularly at church and devoting herself to many charities. It is her last, most successful piece of acting.

At a bazaar, the main characters of the novel meet each other for a moment unexpectedly. Becky, working at a charity booth, looks up and smiles demurely, while Dobbin, Amelia, and their children shrink back at the sight of her. Thus the novel ends in a setting perfectly appropriate to its title, *Vanity Fair*.

NOTES AND GLOSSARY:

'We must have the bones in ...': the Major is threatening to reveal things about Rebecca ('I'll split') unless she helps him to cheat Jos at dice ('the bones')

'Un biglietto ...': (*Italian*) 'Write a letter?—here it is' Becky is singing a song from *The Barber of Seville* (1816) by Rossini (1792–1868). Figaro, the barber, has been trying to persuade the heroine of the opera to write a letter to the man she loves; first she coyly refuses, but in these words she reveals that she had already done so

Vanitas vanitatum: (*Latin*) Vanity of vanities

Part 3

Commentary

The characters

Like the other great panoramic novels of the nineteenth century, *Vanity Fair* creates its effect and expresses its meaning primarily through its characters. Each major character in the novel is entertaining and instructive in his or her own way; each poses a different set of critical problems.

Becky Sharp

Probably the most memorable character in *Vanity Fair* is Becky Sharp. In his introductory chapter, 'Before the Curtain', Thackeray remarks that readers of the novel had admired Becky for being 'flexible' and 'lively'. She is certainly a most energetic, resilient character. Becky starts with little or nothing but her brains and good looks, and she nearly succeeds in winning a place at the top of society. Of course, a careful reader soon realises that her attempt to scale the social heights is bound to fail. A rhythm is built up in the novel, in which we see Becky almost reach a goal, only to have it slip beyond her reach at the last moment. The first major example of this rhythm at work is her unsuccessful attempt to capture Jos as her husband; next she marries Rawdon only to discover that had she waited she could have married Sir Pitt. We come to expect to see her fail in increasingly spectacular ways, until the great, climactic scene occurs when Rawdon discovers her alone with Lord Steyne.

We admire Becky's energy all the more because we realise that she will never succeed. It requires great resilience to keep on trying. Becky thinks of taking her life after Rawdon discovers her with Steyne; a weaker character might do so, but we know that she will not. Even the 'despair' which the narrator tells us overtakes her during her wanderings on the continent (Chapter 64) lasts only for a short time. It is impossible not to feel some sympathy for her when we realise that she cannot fulfil her wishes partly because of the simple accident of her low birth. Why should someone so bright, accomplished, and energetic have to scheme continually to obtain the same things that other people possess simply because their parents are wealthy?

We admire Becky's energy, intelligence, and persistence, and we are bound to feel some sympathy for her plight as a poor girl trying to make a place for herself in the world. Some readers go farther than this, and praise her unreservedly. Her cruelty and deceitfulness are the results of her explosive, 'amoral' energy and resourcefulness. If she does destructive things, the fault is not hers, but society's, for society has put her in the position in which she finds herself in the first place.

What does Thackeray want us to think of Becky? This is a question which each reader must answer for himself or herself, taking into account Becky's actions throughout the novel and Thackeray's comments about them. The evidence is not always simple or obvious. We need to read the novel carefully, to examine Thackeray's commentary with particular reference to its tone (is he being straightforward or ironic in his praise or blame?), to compare a character's words and thoughts with his or her actions.

Becky's admirers defend her, for instance, by pointing to an episode toward the end of the novel. When Becky shows Amelia the letter which George had written on the eve of the battle of Waterloo, she seems to be acting entirely out of a wish to free Amelia from her illusions about her dead husband and convince her that she should marry Dobbin. The action seems the more generous, since Becky knows that Dobbin is her enemy and would separate her from Jos and Amelia if he could.

There is no doubt that Becky's action here makes us feel kindly toward her. There are very few unselfish acts in *Vanity Fair,* and here we seem to have found one. But careful reading casts a shadow over such conclusions, though it does not destroy them altogether. Thackeray makes us doubt the purity of Becky's motives in two main ways. First, he tells us that Becky had thought of her plan to help Dobbin several weeks before she went through with it. Becky forgot about it for the time being because she was too involved in pursuing her own interests: 'Whatever Becky's private plan might be by which Dobbin's true love was to be crowned with success, the little woman thought that the secret might keep, and indeed, being by no means so much interested about anybody's welfare as about her own, she had a great number of things pertaining to herself to consider, and which concerned her a great deal more than Major Dobbin's happiness in this life' (Chapter 67). This hardly makes Becky seem an unselfish person. And in the light of this comment, we begin to wonder whether Becky does not have a reason for remembering her plan when she does. After she has captivated Jos, it is in her interest to get Amelia out of the way. What better way to do so than by promoting a marriage between Amelia and Dobbin? In the event, Dobbin and Amelia leave for England to be married, while

Jos stays behind with Becky, who is now able to gain complete control over his actions. This is not to say that Becky does not show a streak of generosity in helping Amelia over her illusions concerning George. On the other hand, it is significant that Thackeray does not allow even this most attractive, selfless act on Becky's part to gain our unqualified admiration.

Other examples of the way in which Thackeray forces us to judge Becky negatively include her treatment of Amelia, and above all her alienation from her husband and young son. It is a nice touch to give Becky a growing contempt for Rawdon, just when we as readers begin to feel sympathy toward him because of his affection for young Rawdon. Becky's treatment of the child is chilling. How can one forget the picture of the little boy, standing at the foot of the stairs as he listens rapturously to his mother's singing, only to have her suddenly open the door, discover him, and slap him in the face for spying on her?

Becky, then, is not amoral but immoral in most of what she does. Becky is immensely entertaining to watch, but when Lady Jane attacks her for bringing misery and dissension into happy families, she is stating the truth. For all her energy and wit, Becky is destructive, selfish, and ultimately evil. Now the reader may not agree with this assessment; many readers have not. The main thing is that the student of *Vanity Fair* should be able to produce evidence of the sort which has been briefly presented above in support of his or her opinion on this or any other interpretation of Thackeray's text.

Amelia Sedley

Amelia raises a set of rather different problems. In creating her, Thackeray seems to be examining critically one sort of social and fictional stereotype of feminine virtue. It is difficult to know exactly how to feel about Amelia. On the one hand, Thackeray's narrator often gushes over her gentleness and naivety with great delight, especially in the early part of the novel. On the other hand, there is the superb scene in which Dobbin tells Amelia that she is not worthy of him precisely because of the qualities which we are earlier invited to admire in her. She is capable of a passive, steadfast, clinging affection, but nothing more:

'I know what your heart is capable of: it can cling faithfully to a recollection, and cherish a fancy; but it can't feel such an attachment as mine deserves to mate with, and such as I would have won from a woman more generous than you. No, you are not worthy of the love which I have devoted to you. I knew all along that the prize I had set my life on was not worth the winning; that I was a fool, with fond fancies, too, bartering away my all of truth and ardour against your little feeble remnant of love. I will bargain no more: I withdraw. I find no fault with you. You are very good natured, and have done your best; but you couldn't—you couldn't reach up to the height of the attachment which I bore you, and which a loftier soul than yours might have been proud to share' (Chapter 66).

Which version of Amelia should we accept? The idea that she is a self-denying, weak, gentle, perfectly loyal wife and mother, or the view that Dobbin so unforgettably expresses?

Some readers have felt that Thackeray is simply confused, perhaps because the standards of his time invited him to admire in Amelia qualities of which his own best judgement disapproved. Thackeray seems to the present writer anything but confused in the way in which he presents Amelia. The narrator expresses his approval of Amelia most strongly in the opening chapters of the novel; his later effusions involve more pity than praise. Thackeray sets Amelia up as an ideal and then gradually shows her flaws. We come to understand her more and more fully, just as Dobbin does. Even some of Thackeray's best critics have acted as if Dobbin's attack mirrors an unexpected reversal of opinion on Thackeray's part, but this is simply not true. Amelia, like most of Thackeray's characters, has both good and bad qualities. She is gentle and trusting; she tries to be a good wife and mother; she is extraordinarily patient in nursing her father and mother through their old age. On the other hand, she has her faults, and we become gradually aware of them long before Dobbin confronts her with them. From the beginning we may suspect that she is a bit dim and far too passive. Her blind worship of her husband and son is based at least partly on pride. And her treatment of Dobbin is unjust and egotistical. She is not above enjoying the power she has over him and wanting to give him nothing in return for it. Indeed, one of the reasons why the fight between them over whether Becky ought to be taken into Jos's household becomes so ugly is that Amelia is used to ordering Dobbin about and is not prepared to see him rebel from her authority. When Dobbin's attack on Amelia finally comes, we are more than prepared for it: we want to see it happen.

Thackeray's presentation of Amelia, then, seems at least to this reader not a sign of confusion, but one of the clearest proofs of his narrative art in *Vanity Fair*. Authors have always found it easy to make evil attractive. To make us share a growing perception of the weaknesses of a good character like Amelia is a rarer achievement.

William Dobbin

Dobbin is the most admirable major character in the novel. He would be its hero if everything about him were not so decisively unheroic. He is a nice contrast to the 'pushers' in the novel, to characters such as the brilliantly ambitious Becky or the dully obstinate Mr Osborne. But even Dobbin is not without his faults and his own kind of selfishness. He hastens the marriage between Amelia and George Osborne for his own sake as well as for theirs. He wishes to get the pain of seeing the woman he loves marry another man over as quickly as possible. He also deceives himself about Amelia, forming in his imagination a picture of her that is as superior to her as he himself is. Dobbin's selfishness is nevertheless minute compared to that of most of the other characters in the novel, and at least he comes to know that he has been fooling himself about Amelia: '"No," William thought again and again, "it was myself I deluded, and persisted in cajoling; had she been worthy of the love I gave her, she would have returned it long ago. It was a fond mistake. Isn't the whole course of life made up of such? and suppose I had won her, should I not have been disenchanted the day after my victory? Why pine, or be ashamed of my defeat?"' (Chapter 67). So that at least he marries her with open eyes. Thackeray sums up Dobbin's character by describing him as the only true gentleman in the novel: 'He had very long legs, a yellow face, and a slight lisp, which at first was rather ridiculous. But his thoughts were just, his brains were fairly good, his life was honest and pure, and his heart warm and humble' (Chapter 62).

Rawdon Crawley and Pitt Crawley

Most of the characters in *Vanity Fair* have fixed personalities. Rawdon Crawley is exceptional, for he grows and changes morally. When he first appears, he is a stupid, good-natured soldier, fond of women, horses, and gambling. By the end of the novel he is a sympathetic human being, capable of attempting a moral stand against Becky and Lord Steyne. His growth is brought about by his love for his young son.

Pitt Crawley is different. Outwardly, he transforms himself from a strait-laced bigot into an ambitious politician; inwardly, he changes not at all. Instead, like most of the other characters in *Vanity Fair*, Pitt adapts his unchanging personality to new conditions. When he is at Queen's Crawley at the beginning of the novel, he is a man temporarily disappointed of a public career; his religiosity is primarily a means by which he can assert his own dignity and win his father's uneasy respect.

When circumstances change, his ambition shows itself and his fundamentalism recedes: it is no longer necessary and indeed has become an encumbrance.

Pitt is a cold, rather unpleasant character, but Thackeray gives him some redeeming features. When he inherits his father's baronetcy and becomes Sir Pitt Crawley, he decides 'to rule justly and honestly, to depose Lady Southdown, and to be on the friendliest possible terms with all the relations of his blood' (Chapter 40). Despite the comic touch of Pitt's decision to escape the tyranny of his mother-in-law Lady Southdown, we feel a real if frigid decency here. Later, when Rawdon comes to Pitt after he has discovered Becky and Steyne together, we find the same mixture of qualities. Pitt is terrified that Rawdon will try to borrow money from him, but when he learns that what Rawdon wants is someone to take care of his son, he generously accepts the responsibility.

Jos Sedley

Jos Sedley is the comic stereotype of a wealthy Anglo-Indian, with his love of Indian food, resulting corpulence, and long stories about adventures in India which turn out to be lies. This element of stock comedy, as well as his despicable cowardice in leaving Amelia to her fate in Brussels when he thinks that the French are coming, both ensure that we do not develop much sympathy for Jos. He remains primarily the butt of our laughter. This lack of sympathy is useful to Thackeray toward the end of the novel. He can broadly suggest that Becky has actually murdered Jos without making us lose all sympathy for her. Imagine if there were a hint that she had murdered a character like Dobbin, or Amelia, or even Rawdon Crawley! Thackeray obtains from the suggestion that Becky may be a murderess a final reminder of the ruthless side of her character. And the dramatic, polar disparity between the picture of Becky as a murderess and our final view of Becky at the charity booth perfectly sums up the contradictions in her character and situation which are apparent throughout the novel. If we took Jos seriously, if he were not a comic stereotype, Thackeray could not produce these striking effects.

Other stock characters

Thackeray's early work as a literary parodist, who imitated in a comically exaggerated way the styles of other authors, made him acutely aware of the limitations and distortions inherent in literary conventions, especially those that had become clichés. He attacks a number of such conventions in *Vanity Fair*, for example accepted notions of what fictional heroes should be like. The intention is to create a fiction closer to reality, less a vehicle for the reader's fantasies about life, more a mirror of society as it actually exists.

Thackeray nevertheless finds it convenient to base some of his characters on stock characters used again and again by earlier authors. Perhaps the most obvious of these are Bute Crawley, the fox-hunting parson, and his son, the idle undergraduate. Mr Paul Jefferson Jones is another, minor example of this sort of character. He is an American journalist who appears briefly, and who, like most American journalists in nineteenth-century British fiction (*Martin Chuzzlewit*, by Dickens, provides several examples) has bad manners, writes in a pompous and stupid way, and misunderstands everything British. Less pleasant is the portrayal of Miss Swartz, the stereotypic mulatto heiress from the West Indies, with her woolly hair and absurd overdressing. Then there are Peggy O'Dowd and her sister Glorvina, with their love of Irish melodies and everything else Irish, and their exaggerated accents and modes of speech.

We enjoy such characters not because they tell us everything about life or even because they capture the essence of a certain kind of person (for in fact they rarely do so), but because they have characteristics at which we are used to laughing. Change, growth, or depth in such characters would be utterly inappropriate. In this they are like famous cartoon figures. Donald Duck does not need to change or reveal his soul to us—he merely needs to be himself, and we will laugh.

A slightly different sort of stereotyped caricature-character is Mr Bullock, who eventually marries Mr Osborne's younger daughter, with his comic use of financial language for every occasion: he talks of 'making a bid' for the heiress Miss Swartz (that is, proposing to her) and of being 'booked' (that is, engaged) to Miss Osborne.

'Good' characters: Briggs and Lady Jane

Thackeray's stock characters are very funny in their way. A gentler kind of humour, mixed with a slight melancholy, is provided by other characters in the novel. The actions of the few unselfish people in *Vanity Fair* often evoke in the reader a half-pitying, half-admiring smile. This is particularly true of Briggs. Briggs becomes comically jealous with Becky for taking her place as Miss Crawley's nurse, but her naturally gentle, yielding nature makes her forgive Becky completely. Utterly guileless, she allows herself to be hired by Becky later in the novel, and even lends Becky the small inheritance left her by Miss Crawley. She is saved from ruin only because Rawdon, who is grateful for the way in which she has taken care of young Rawdon, makes his brother Pitt promise to repay the debt with part of the money Rawdon has discovered that Becky was hiding from him.

Briggs's gentle nature comes from early suffering. Earlier in life, she was in love with a writing-master who apparently died young. Her memories of him are a delicious mixture of the comic and the genuinely touching:

> 'Poor thing, poor thing!' says Briggs (who was thinking of twenty-four years back, and that hectic young writing-master whose lock of yellow hair, and whose letters, beautiful in their illegibility, she cherished in her old desk upstairs). 'Poor thing, poor thing!' says Briggs. Once more she was a fresh-cheeked lass of eighteen; she was at evening church, and the hectic writing-master and she were quavering out of the same psalm-book (Chapter 15).

Thackeray's ability to evoke the world of memory in a few short lines is extraordinary; it is one of his greatest gifts.

Something of this gentle humour hovers around Lady Jane when she first appears in the novel. Like Briggs, she is a character lovable for her naivety, and for the way in which, though completely dominated by her mother (as Briggs is dominated by Miss Crawley), she nonetheless preserves her own freshness and ability to love. There is a charming moment when poor Lady Jane, used to her puritanical mother's notions about the impropriety of playing card-games of any kind, brings herself to admit to Miss Crawley that she used to make her father happy by playing piquet with him on the sly:

> Lady Jane blushed to the tips of her little ears, and down to the ends of her pretty fingers; and when Mr Bowls had quitted the room and the door was quite shut, she said—'Miss Crawley, I can play [cards] a little. I used to—to play a little with poor dear papa.'

Miss Crawley's reaction is the same as the reader's: she calls Lady Jane a 'dear good little soul' (Chapter 34).

In time, Lady Jane loses her naivety, but she gains an impressive moral stature. Like Dobbin, she comes to see Becky for what she is and makes a stand against her. Lady Jane discovers Becky's true nature when her love for children leads her to discover that Becky has neglected young Rawdon, another of the novel's 'good' characters, who after his own early sufferings is lucky enough to have Lady Jane to act as his mother. Young Rawdon is a moral touchstone in the novel. He causes his father's growth into a sympathetic human being, and it is appropriate that both Lady Jane and Briggs love and protect the boy.

Rich merchants: the Osbornes and the Sedleys

One of the great achievements of *Vanity Fair* is its portrait of the London merchant class, which comes to life most fully in the Osborne family. The verdict is hardly favourable. Old Osborne is full of self-importance, a bully to his family, a man who will never admit that he is wrong. He is without pity toward his old friend and benefactor Mr Sedley when the latter's business fails. His son George is thoroughly selfish. His daughters abandon their brother to Osborne's wrath when they realize that if George is disinherited, there will be more money for them. The narrator sums up the family as a whole (with the possible exception of Osborne's down-trodden older daughter) when he says of Mr Osborne: 'Always to be right, always to trample forward, and never to doubt, are not these the great qualities with which dulness takes the lead in the world?' (Chapter 35). Yet for all of this, Thackeray is able to make us feel and pity old Osborne's suffering when he disinherits his son.

At the beginning of the novel, Mr Sedley seems much like Mr Osborne. Sedley enjoys cruel practical jokes, as when he persuades Becky to try some very hot Indian food. He is also crafty and alert, and quickly recognizes that Becky has designs on Jos. Sedley's ruin is a reminder of the hollowness of this sort of life. His wife's once genial temper is permanently soured by poverty. All that is left to Sedley himself is to hate Osborne, grumble at his fate, dream of the past, and make fruitless attempts to regain his fortune. Only at the end of his life, with death drawing near, does he allow himself to admit defeat, to relax and find some happiness in the loving attention of his daughter.

Wicked aristocrats: Sir Pitt, Lord Steyne, and Miss Crawley

Thackeray's portrait of the Regency aristocracy is nearly as full and satisfying as his presentation of the commercial classes. Some—the Bareacres, for instance—are simply dull and self-important. But the aristocrats who stand out in our minds after finishing the novel are more positively wicked.

Sir Pitt Crawley begins as a literary joke. Thackeray takes the picture of a Baronet one might find in genteel fiction and reverses it. Instead of being young, handsome, polite, refined, and generous, Sir Pitt is ageing, ugly, rude, coarse, and a miser. But Sir Pitt soon becomes more than a piece of literary wit. Thackeray portrays him in a way that makes him believable and helps to show how he and his forebears have maintained their power. Reprobate though he is, Sir Pitt makes certain that the best family jewels go not to the lower-class Miss Horrocks but to Lady Jane, the wife of the future Baronet of Queen's Crawley. He may be slovenly and penny-pinching, but he knows how to maintain the respect of his inferiors: 'boor as he was, Sir Pitt was a stickler for his dignity while at home, and seldom drove out but with four horses, and though he dined off boiled mutton, had always three footmen to serve it' (Chapter 9). Thackeray tells us that 'the whole baronetage, peerage, commonage of England, did not contain a more cunning, mean, selfish, foolish, disreputable old man' (Chapter 9). Yet Sir Pitt has his own kind of dignity, which comes from his vitality and resilience, qualities that would have made him an interesting mate for Becky and which lead him to try to win her against social convention and in spite of the difference of their ages.

Sir Pitt Crawley's half-sister, Miss Crawley, seems very unlike her brother in her refined tastes, but the two have much in common. Miss Crawley enjoys a good fight just as much as Sir Pitt does, only instead of engaging in lawsuits, she sets her prospective heirs against one another. Like Sir Pitt, though in a less flagrant way, Miss Crawley is willing to flirt with the lower classes. She likes to think of herself as a radical in politics and a believer in equality. Thus on a number of occasions she tells Becky that Becky deserves to be an aristocrat because she has more brains than most women with titles have. But when faced with a concrete situation, Miss Crawley like Sir Pitt instinctively and absolutely sides with her own class. She disowns Rawdon for marrying Becky just as surely as Sir Pitt prevents the best family jewels from going to Miss Horrocks.

There is finally Lord Steyne, much more powerful and considerably more wicked than either Sir Pitt or his half-sister. Lord Steyne raises in a particularly dramatic way the question of Thackeray's attitude toward life. For some of the most unpleasant visions of human existence in nineteenth-century fiction are connected with Lord Steyne as well as with Thackeray's other wicked aristocrats. Steyne never knows when madness will wrench him from his place of power and influence and cast him into a madhouse, for there is a strain of hereditary insanity in the family. One day his younger son suddenly went insane, and the description of his life, secreted away in one of Steyne's country houses, laughing hysterically, playing with dolls, whimpering, sometimes remembering and sometimes forgetting who his mother is when she visits him secretly—such a description implies a mordant view of life and its possibilities indeed. The depiction of Sir Pitt Crawley's last days, when he is paralysed and helpless, has something of the same flavour:

> Lady Jane always walked by the old man [when he was taken out in a chair]; and was an evident favourite with him. He used to nod many times to her and smile when she came in, and utter inarticulate deprecatory moans when she was going away. When the door shut upon her he would cry and sob—whereupon [his nurse] Hester's face and manner, which was always exceedingly bland and gentle while her lady was present, would change at once, and she would make faces at him and clench her fist, and scream out, 'Hold your tongue, you stoopid old fool,' and twirl away his chair from the fire which he loved to look at—at which he would cry more. For this was all that was left after more than seventy years of cunning and struggling, and drinking, and scheming, and sin and selfishness—a whimpering old idiot put in and out of bed and cleaned and fed like a baby (Chapter 40).

Now, one reason why these terrible scenes exist is to underline a proposition stated several times in the novel—that even the most exalted members of society may not be so fortunate as they seem. Maria Osborne may be rich and respectable, but her life with her father is torture. Lord Steyne may possess enormous power and live in splendour, but insanity is lurking around the corner. Yet the pictures of Steyne's insane younger son and of Sir Pitt is his dotage seem excessively cruel and frightening if their purpose is merely to point out that the rich and powerful have problems, just as the rest of us do. Do these scenes reflect something more negative about Thackeray's vision of life?

Narrative technique

The plot

Vanity Fair has been accused of formlessness. It certainly lacks the elegant design of novels which are more firmly focused on the progress of a single main character. Unlike such novels, *Vanity Fair* is organised around the lives of two characters, Becky and Amelia, and there are long stretches in the novel where the activities of each woman have little or no direct effect on the other. Hence the novel's plot may not seem to form an integrated whole.

But the two lines of action in *Vanity Fair* form their own kind of unity, though it is not the tight, logical unity we find in a plot built around a single main character. There is a rough contrast in the fortunes of the two main characters: when Becky's fortunes rise, Amelia's tend to fall and vice-versa. Both women also face similar situations at the same time during the novel. When they meet in Brussels, for instance, both of their husbands have been disinherited. But the deepest unity in the novel arises from the fact that its characters are driven by the same basic impulses. They all live in Vanity Fair.

The narrator

We have not yet mentioned Thackeray's most remarkable character of all—his narrator. As soon as we begin reading *Vanity Fair*, we are aware of a voice, describing things, judging them, adding personal comments and anecdotes, questioning our own reactions and even our motives. All novels have some sort of narrative presence, express or implied: the story must after all be told by someone. What is distinctive about Thackeray's narrator is that he is so visible, so obviously there.

Sometimes the narrator talks directly to us, asking us questions or sharing his own experiences with us. In creating this sort of narrative voice, Thackeray is following a great eighteenth-century tradition in English fiction: one thinks of the narrators of Fielding's *Tom Jones* (1749) or Sterne's *Tristram Shandy* (1760-7). Reading this sort of novel becomes a conversation between us and the author, sometimes genial, sometimes not. There are some delightful, essentially light-hearted passages of this kind in *Vanity Fair*, particularly in the opening chapters. Thus the narrator tells us what one of his audience must be thinking as he reads the details of how Amelia's friends weep and wail when she leaves school:

> All which details, I have no doubt, JONES, who reads this book at his Club, will pronounce to be excessively foolish, trivial, twaddling, and ultra-sentimental. Yes; I can see Jones at this minute (rather flushed with his joint of mutton and half-pint of wine) taking out his pencil and scoring under the words 'foolish, twaddling' etc., and adding to them his own remark of '*quite true.*' Well, he is a lofty man of genius, and admires the great and heroic in life and novels; and so had better take warning and go elsewhere (Chapter 1).

This is a shrewd way of winning our sympathy for the scene (*we* do not want to be like Jones) as well as letting us know that Thackeray knows that he is being sentimental. But often, especially as the novel progresses, these direct addresses to the reader become more serious and even hostile. There is, for instance, the following challenge: 'O brother wearers of motley! Are there not moments when one grows sick of grinning and tumbling, and the jingling of cap and bells? This, dear friends and companions, is my amiable object—to walk with you through the Fair, to examine the shops and the shows there; and that we should all come home after the flare, and the noise, and the gaiety, and be perfectly miserable in private' (Chapter 19). Perhaps the main function of the narrator's conversation with us is to remind us that we too live in Vanity Fair.

A second kind of narrative presence is more objective. The narrator does not seek to engage us in conversation; instead, he makes short, pithy statements about what he is describing, such as the following: 'Which of the dead are most tenderly and passionately deplored? Those who love the survivors the least, I believe' (Chapter 61). This remark gains its authority because we have seen such striking examples of love unworthily bestowed (Amelia's love for George, for instance) and love taken for granted (Dobbin's love for Amelia, for example). Such moral commentary as the narrator gives usually states in the form of a generalization an idea that has already been acted out before us by the novel's characters. It is not a substitute for direct, fictional enactment.

The narrator makes his presence known in more subtle ways as well, which do not involve extended or overt addresses to the reader. Sometimes a single word or phrase reveals that he is not simply presenting but is also evaluating a scene or character. The following passage, which describes how young Rawdon goes away to school, may serve as an example:

It was *honest* Briggs who made up the little kit for the boy which he was to take to school ... *Mrs* Becky could not let her husband have the carriage to take the boy to school ... She was chattering and laughing with a score of young dandies by the Serpentine, as the father and son entered the old gates of the school—where Rawdon left the child, and came away with a sadder purer feeling in his heart than perhaps that *poor battered fellow* had ever known since he himself came out of the nursery* (Chapter 52).

The words italicized in this passage make us feel that the narrator is judging the scene, not simply presenting it. We can tell that he finds Briggs and Rawdon admirable, Becky callous. When the narrator calls Becky 'Mrs Becky,' for instance, he is underlining the conclusion which we reach simply from seeing her actions. The narrator reminds us that Becky is a wife and mother (*Mrs* Becky), even though, by flirting with other men while her husband takes their son away to school, she acts as if she were not.

*Italics added by present author.

In reacting to the narrator's judgements, direct or implied, it is helpful to remember that there is always at least a potential difference between Thackeray as author on the one hand, and the narrator of *Vanity Fair* on the other. Thackeray has created the narrative voice just as much as he has created any other character in the novel. The narrator need not directly express Thackeray's own opinions, any more than Dobbin does or Becky does. Sometimes the narrator does so, sometimes not.

Objections to Thackeray's narrator

Some readers object to Thackeray's narrator. They find him distracting. Just when our imagination becomes involved in the novel sufficiently for it to seem lifelike, they complain, the narrator intrudes himself and reminds us that we are reading a book. Thackeray's characters should act out his meaning directly; the novel would be more imaginatively powerful if they did. There ought to be no need for his narrative comments. This criticism of the narrator is part of a larger complaint that Thackeray does not take his characters seriously enough. The metaphor which he uses to describe his relationship to them at the opening and the close of the novel is said to be a case in point. He calls them puppets; he himself is the puppet-master. But this is the worst possible way to conceive of fictional characters, his critics say. Characters in a novel should not be puppets. The writer should do his best to make them real, independent, living men and women, which means (among other things) that he himself should never act as if he is controlling what they do. Instead, he should disappear, leaving them alone on the stage to act out their own lives.

There is something to be said for this objection. In some novels we do forget the narrator, and the characters do seem to act out their lives before us as if they were living men and women. Sometimes we feel this way when reading *Vanity Fair*, but probably not very often. On the other hand, would we really like all of our novels to create the same sort of experience? It is a mistake to think that Thackeray might merely have added greater dramatic force to his novel, like an extra layer to a cake. If he sacrificed the narrator's overt presence, he would sacrifice much that is best about his work.

Though Thackeray's style of narration may preclude a certain kind of dramatic vividness, it has its strengths as well. Our dialogue with the narrator continually makes us revise our opinions about characters and events, and in this way makes us experience the difficulty of making moral judgements. The narrator, who is always ready to interrupt the onward flow of the story with information about the past or speculations about the future, is responsible for one of the novel's distinctive achievements—the way it makes us feel the passing of time and the richness of memory. Perhaps it is better to enjoy *Vanity Fair* for what it is, instead of condemning it for not being quite a different sort of book from the one which Thackeray intended to write. The narrator is in other words an integral part of the special world that Thackeray creates in *Vanity Fair*.

The world of *Vanity Fair*

'A Novel without a Hero'

The subtitle of *Vanity Fair* provides a convenient way to discuss the world that Thackeray depicts in the novel. When he calls his work 'A Novel without a Hero,' Thackeray is suggesting a number of things on a number of levels. On a purely literary level, he is making an indirect attack on conventional novels. *His* novel, he seems to be saying, contains real men and women, not unrealistic heroes and heroines with super-human passions, impossible virtues, and unbelievable trials and tribulations. In a larger sense, the subtitle is intended to make us re-evaluate our conception of heroes and the heroic. One of Thackeray's achievements is to make us share Amelia's discovery that George Osborne, who by right of his good looks and dashing manner ought to be a hero in a novel, is in fact far inferior to the utterly unheroic-looking William Dobbin.

Some readers have seen in the novel's subtitle a sly suggestion that while there may not be any hero in the novel, there is certainly a heroine—Becky Sharp. The narrator at one point takes this line himself. When he describes Becky's heartless indifference to the fact that Rawdon is on his way to the battle of Waterloo, the narrator states that:

> If this is a novel without a hero, at least let us lay claim to a heroine. No man in the British army which has marched away, not the great Duke himself, could be more cool or collected in the presence of doubts and difficulties, than the indomitable little aide-de-camp's wife [that is, Becky] (Chapter 30).

Before taking this statement too seriously, it is well to recall an earlier passage which claimed that Amelia was the heroine of *Vanity Fair* because she possessed just the opposite qualities from those which now supposedly make Becky the heroine. The narrator talks of 'the heroine of this work, Miss Sedley (whom we have selected for the very reason that she was the best-natured of all . . .)' (Chapter 2). When Thackeray nominates Becky as his hero, he is being ironic about her cold and calculating nature, and at the same time criticising the idea that true heroism involves the military virtues which Becky displays. As for Amelia, it is an odd heroine indeed who can be told by an unheroic male like Dobbin that she is unworthy of him.

Why are there no heroes or heroines in *Vanity Fair*? One reason involves Thackeray's recognition of human weakness. If we look back at the gallery of characters in *Vanity Fair*, we can see that the best of them are touched, and the worst of them dominated, by one overriding failing—selfishness. The lust for social status which fills so many of Thackeray's characters is a selfish drive; it thrives at the expense of others. Thackeray's very best characters are less self-serving, but just because they are self-effacing instead of egotistical, they are usually dominated by their more selfish fellows. Lady Jane is completely led by the nose by her mother when she is a girl; through most of the novel Dobbin does everything he can for Amelia and receives nothing in return. And even Dobbin is not entirely free from the ruling fault of selfishness. As we have seen, his concern for his own feelings helps to make him hasten the marriage between George and Amelia.

Thackeray's sense of human weakness, then, is too strong to allow him to portray a set of perfectly good characters in *Vanity Fair*. But there is another reason why the novel lacks a hero. The world in which the characters live precludes action that would be heroic in the sense of being simple, decisive and satisfying.

Here we approach the heart of the novel. Dobbin, the character who comes closest to being heroic, also has the clearest insight into the unheroic nature of the world in which he lives. Here is how he talks about his love for Amelia when he believes that he has lost her: 'It was a fond mistake. Isn't the whole course of life made up of such? and suppose I had won her, should I not have been disenchanted the day after my victory?' (Chapter 67). The narrator's closing words in the novel sound the same note. 'Which of us is happy in this world? Which of us has his desire? or, having it, is satisfied?' (Chapter 67). We expect the actions of a hero to be capped by a grand success or a magnificent failure. In the world of *Vanity Fair* we find instead—anti-climax. *Vanity Fair* as a whole can be seen as an extended dramatisation which acts out Dobbin's perception that our goals, even when we reach them, never prove equal to our expectations. The rhythm which controls Becky's destiny is a perfect example of this law, for even when she gains the goals which she has set for herself (for instance, marrying Rawdon), she finds them incomplete, unsatisfactory, or (as in the case of mingling with the highest society in England) ultimately boring. Any reader of the novel ought to be able to provide many other examples of this sort for Becky and for the other characters—think of Mr Osborne's dealings with his son, for instance. The attack on conventional literature implied by the idea of writing a novel without a hero falls into place here also. One of the ways in whiċh the vast majority of novels conventionally lie about life is in the way they usually end, as the narrator's comment on Amelia's disappointment after her marriage with George makes clear:

'Was the prize gained—the heaven of life—and the winner still doubtful and unsatisfied? As his hero and heroine pass the matrimonial barrier, the novelist generally drops the curtain, as if the drama were over then: the doubts and struggles of life ended: as if, once landed in the marriage country, all were green and pleasant there: and wife and husband had nothing to do but to link each other's arms together, and wander gently downwards towards old age in happy and perfect fruition. But our little Amelia was just on the bank of her new country, and was already looking anxiously back towards the sad friendly figures waving farewell to her across the stream, from the other distant shore' (Chapter 26).

'And they lived happily ever after,' Thackeray is saying, may be a good ending for a fairy tale, but it is a false ending for any novel that aims to depict life as it is lived by real men and women.

The deepest reasons, then, why *Vanity Fair* is a novel without a hero are both individual and social. Even the best human beings are too selfish to be morally heroic, and social reality is such that clean-cut, satisfyingly heroic action is impossible anyway. Such a view of life is certainly bleak. It is also one reason why, at least in certain moods, we feel that Thackeray is a novelist who tells the truth about life.

Vanity Fair as social criticism

Does the lack of heroic action in *Vanity Fair* stem from the qualities of the specific society Thackeray depicts, or is it an expression of a more general truth about the situation in which men find themselves in all human societies?

Some critics take the view that the true subject of *Vanity Fair* is a specific society, British industrial society in the nineteenth century. Thackeray's characters, the argument goes, are the products of a certain stage of social development. Their destructive self-seeking reflects the selfishness of industrial capitalism. Becky Sharp is fated to pursue rank and wealth relentlessly, because she lives in a society in which money and social status are the only real values. She is an example of what is wrong with nineteenth-century England.

To some extent, this line of criticism seems valid. *Vanity Fair* does indeed give us the impression of a particular kind of society. It is clear enough that Thackeray feels deep anger at many of the aspects of the society around him. The spectacle of Mr Osborne hounding his friend and benefactor Mr Sedley is maddening in its injustice.

There is a good deal of social criticism in *Vanity Fair*. But if we assume that making a critique of social wrongs is Thackeray's primary purpose in the novel, grave problems begin to arise. It is significant that those critics who are most committed to seeing *Vanity Fair* as social criticism often find the novel unsatisfactory. They usually find themselves wanting to write a new novel, using some of the materials which Thackeray has created. In this revised version, Becky would be unquestionably the heroine. We would admire her as a social rebel, or perhaps we would pity her as a person irretrievably damaged by the society around her. At any rate, she would be the centre of our attention, since she is the most efficient device in *Vanity Fair* for criticising society at large. With this elevation of Becky would go a corresponding shift in emphasis away from Amelia and Dobbin, for what do they have to tell us about industrial capitalism? Perhaps they ought not to be in the novel at all.

If we are primarily interested in understanding *Vanity Fair* as Thackeray actually wrote it, we will probably resist this attack on everything in the novel which does not coincide with a given critic's vision of nineteenth-century society and its ills, however profound or humane that vision might be. Thackeray cares about his contemporary world, and he is angry at its inhumanity, but his ultimate concern lies elsewhere. The specific society depicted in *Vanity Fair* serves to dramatise the vanity of human wishes in any society. The novel's social satire is interesting, pointed, and effective, but it is not the key to the meaning of the work as a whole.

Vanity Fair as a criticism of life

Most readers would agree that *Vanity Fair* contains a characteristic vision of human life. The entire novel can be considered as an extended dramatisation of the proposition 'Which of us is happy in this world? Which of us has his desire? or, having it, is satisfied?' with which the novel ends. But can we say that *Vanity Fair* is more than simply a picture or dramatisation? Is it a comment, an analysis, a criticism of life as well? Does the novel simply embody a despairing vision of life's shortcomings, or does it also imply a set of positive values?

Some readers believe that the vision of life expressed in *Vanity Fair* is merely negative. They have a good deal of evidence for this claim. A few of the narrator's comments may serve as examples. He tells us, for instance, that when Becky visits the Sedley family at the opening of the novel, she and Amelia soon 'loved each other like sisters. Young unmarried girls always do, if they are in a house together for ten days' (Chapter 4). Or we may consider the following, rather more savage remark: 'It is those who injure women who get the most kindness from them—they are born timid and tyrants, and maltreat those who are humblest before them' (Chapter 50). Or the following: 'Did we know what our intimates and our dear relations thought of us, we should live in a world that we should be glad to quit, and in a frame of mind and a constant terror, that would be perfectly unbearable' (Chapter 31). Some readers recoil from this sort of thing, deciding that Thackeray is a misanthrope, a mere critic of humanity with nothing positive to say.

A second view, held by some of our best critics of Thackeray (such as Gordon Ray), finds in *Vanity Fair* a mature, sad, yet accepting vision of human nature and the world. The cynical comments which abound in the novel are said to be balanced by a love of the simple virtues which Dobbin displays, and a sense of the human grandeur inherent in the very act of desiring those things which we cannot attain. Even as decadent a figure as Lord Steyne has his dignity. Such critics would argue that the viewpoint expressed by *Vanity Fair* is not so negative after all.

One reason why we might be reasonably cheerful after reading *Vanity Fair* is that, in the long run, something like justice seems to prevail in the novel. Thackeray does not allow his 'good' characters, those who are least selfish, to be seriously damaged by their life in a vain and heartless world. Briggs, so trusting and so kind to young Rawdon, is not finally cheated out of her savings by Becky. (Becky does ruin her landlord in London, but he had after all involved himself in the general social corruption by assuming that Becky was having an affair with Steyne and relying on the fact that Steyne would pay her debts.) Little Rawdon, after his sad childhood, becomes a Baronet and seems to be living happily with his adopted mother, the admirable Lady Jane. Then there is Dobbin. His illusions about Amelia are shattered, it is true, but he still retains an affection for her. He has his young daughter to love as well, and the 'History of the Punjaub' to occupy his leisure. His is indeed a melancholy yet pleasing life to contemplate.

A third view concentrates less on the novel's effect as a mellow experience created by Thackeray and shared by the reader. Instead the novel is seen as a process of moral education. The seeming contradictions in the narrator's evaluation of the people and events of the novel, as well as his excursions into cynicism or sentimentalism, are considered to be deliberate attempts by Thackeray to make us experience as we read the novel how difficult it is to come to conclusive moral judgements. Thackeray's theme is thus the complexity of the moral world. When, after the great scene when Rawdon discovers Becky and Steyne together, the narrator asks 'Was she guilty?' he is asking a question which the reader comes to realise cannot be answered with certainty. In some ways Becky is guilty; in other ways, she is not. By coming to understand the complexity of moral judgement, we learn compassion and forbearance for our fellow inhabitants of Vanity Fair. Thackeray's insistence on the potential baseness of human nature is not a sign of cynicism or misanthropy; instead it is a sharp reminder to the reader not to judge others too harshly, since human weakness is common to all men and women.

That Thackeray wishes to shake any moral self-righteousness and complacency in his readers seems clear enough from several passages in which he reminds us that we too live in Vanity Fair. After showing us how young George Osborne is selfishly happy to be separated from his mother since it means living in a bigger house and going to a better school, for instance, the narrator reminds us of our own weakness: 'When you think that the eyes of your childhood dried at the sight of a piece of gingerbread, and that a plum-cake was a compensation for the agony of parting with your mamma and sisters; O my friend and brother, you need not be too confident of your own fine feelings' (Chapter 56). We may differ about how 'resigned' or 'cheerful' we find Thackeray's view of the world he has created. In the opinion of the present writer, there is a great deal more of human anguish and even fear in Thackeray's reaction to the human depths which he uncovers than can be adequately described by using such words. The picture of Sir Pitt's infantile weeping as he is mistreated by his sadistic nurse evokes stronger feelings than that. But each reader must decide how to set the balance between the novel's pessimistic, frightening moments on the one hand and its decent respect for the virtues of a William Dobbin on the other. What we can all agree upon is the suggestion that Thackeray's unsparing analysis of the less flattering side of human motivation has or ought to have a chastening effect on the reader. After experiencing *Vanity Fair*, we are indeed unlikely to be 'too confident of our fine feelings'.

Part 4

Hints for study

On writing examinations

Examinations are an inevitable part of the life of most students. Success in writing on a work such as *Vanity Fair* will naturally depend upon a full, accurate, and informed knowledge of Thackeray's text, and it has been the object of this little book to promote such a knowledge. But when the time comes to convey what one has learned to an examiner, there are certain steps that can be taken to make the process as painless and successful as possible.

1. Read the question carefully. It is amazing how often students, eager to begin writing immediately, simply glance at a question, misread it, and write an essay which has little relevance to the assigned topic. The results are usually unfortunate. Take time to read the question carefully.

2. Have a point to make before you start writing. When you are sure that you have understood the assigned question, respond to it with a specific, concrete generalisation. Such a generalisation is called a thesis; it is your answer to the question, the point you will try to prove. Give your essay a title: this is one way to help ensure that your essay has a thesis and is about something specific.

Particularly in a short essay, the best place for your thesis is in the first paragraph. Putting it there reminds you to spend the rest of your time explaining and supporting it. If you have a definite thesis to prove, the problem of organising your answer becomes manageable. If not, your essay is likely to ramble, since it will lack a focus.

3. Take time to plan and organise your essay. The sight of student hands, busily writing two minutes after an examination paper has been distributed, is familiar and disheartening. The most important minutes you spend in an examination are those during which you think about the question, decide on a thesis, and organise examples that will help to prove it. Most students would find it helpful to jot down a rough outline of what they want to say, in the order in which they have decided to say it. Having done so, you can concentrate on making each sentence and paragraph clear to the reader. You will not lose track of your argument in the process of writing: it will be there in front of you, in your rough outline. Students who begin writing immediately may become confused and run out of steam long before the allotted time has expired. This will not happen to you, if you take the time to plan your essay in advance.

4. Use specific, apt examples to prove your thesis. After you have decided upon a thesis, your remaining task is to explain its significance and prove its accuracy by referring to specific characters, incidents, and scenes in the novel. Remember to use examples to make a point; do not simply start re-telling the story for its own sake (or to prove that you have read it). If the assigned question has more than one side, show your reader that you realise this. Cite examples which might seem to disprove your thesis, but then show that the evidence supporting your interpretation of the text is stronger.

5. Write your essay in clear, grammatical English. In the excitement and tension of taking an examination, students sometimes forget about their writing style. If you take five or ten minutes to plan your essay in advance, you will be able to concentrate more fully on producing clear, accurate, interesting prose when you begin to write. If possible, re-read your answer carefully before handing it in.

Most examiners are not primarily interested in whether the answer you write to a question agrees with their own opinion on the subject at hand. Instead, they are looking for evidence that you can read perceptively and write clearly. A well-organised essay, in which you support a reasonable thesis with concrete, apt examples from the text will impress them favourably. An essay which is full of unsupported generalisations, or which simply re-tells the story for no obvious purpose, will not impress them.

Questions and answers

The paragraphs which follow are intended to provide examples of the kinds of questions you might be asked about *Vanity Fair* in an examination, and the ways in which you might go about answering them. In what follows we shall concentrate on the process outlined above—understanding the question, responding to it by forming a thesis about it, and supporting that thesis with apt examples. This will also be a convenient time to review the major critical ideas and interpretations already discussed. The specific critical issues mentioned below are dealt with in detail in the appropriate sections of Part 3: Commentary.

QUESTIONS ON CHARACTERS

Becky Sharp

'Becky is the most interesting and convincingly portrayed character in Vanity Fair.*' Discuss.*

To deal effectively with this sort of question, you need to look carefully at the terms it uses and to make some distinctions. In this case, it is useful to distinguish between various ways in which a character can be 'interesting.' As an isolated character, Becky is indeed probably more interesting than any other person in the novel, in the sense of being intelligent and lively. But in terms of the novel as a whole, you could argue that both Dobbin and Amelia are at least as interesting as Becky, in that they both have much to tell us about the vanity of human wishes, the prevalence of selfishness, and the need for compassion in judging others. The same reasoning can be applied to the term 'convincingly portrayed.' Becky is convincing in her way, but so are the other characters in theirs. The question, in other words, has two sides to it, and a good answer will reflect this.

One possible thesis might run as follows. 'Becky Sharp is indeed an interesting character; we are fascinated by her brilliant attempts to climb the social ladder, by her perseverance and versatility. But there are other characters in *Vanity Fair* who may be less extraordinary as individuals but who are nonetheless more interesting than Becky as expressions of Thackeray's deepest concerns.' Having arrived at this thesis, the task is now to support it. The essay's organisation follows clearly from the thesis. In the first part of the essay, you would describe some of the ways in which Becky is indeed 'interesting and convincingly portrayed.' You could mention the brilliant ease with which she adapts herself to different situations—how she is able to hold her own against Miss Pinkerton at school by speaking French to the old lady; how she makes herself indispensable to Sir Pitt and Miss Crawley, reaches the highest London society, survives even after society has banished her from England, and finally is able to enslave Jos and use his money to gain semi-respectability back in England. In the second part of your essay you would show that other characters in the novel are equally interesting and perhaps even more significant in the development of the theme of the work as a whole than Becky. The range of possible evidence is very large. An obvious example is the way in which Amelia is presented as an utterly convincing specimen of a certain kind of woman; as the novel progresses, the reader comes to realise her shortcomings and those of the literary and social ideals which she represents. You might also mention Rawdon Crawley as an example of convincing moral growth during the novel, or Dobbin, who is the embodiment of what a true gentleman ought to be.

On the other hand, you might agree with the topic completely. If so, you could state your thesis as follows: 'Becky is not the only important character in *Vanity Fair*, but she is the most interesting and convincing character in the novel. Her career sums up both Thackeray's specific criticisms of society and his general view of life.' You would then go on to describe (briefly) the importance of some of the other characters, and to spend the majority of your time discussing Becky's role in the novel.

Notice that in either case, whether you agree or disagree with the question, your essay will reflect your critical understanding of the novel. In both cases, you show that you understand that the question has two sides. Most important, both essays move from a consideration of individual characters to a discussion of their function and significance in the novel as a whole.

Other characters

We have spent a good deal of time on Becky, for the practical reason that she seems the character about whom you are most likely to be asked to write in an examination. Some sample questions concerning the other characters in the novel follow.

'Dobbin and Amelia are unconvincing characters; they are too good and unselfish to be true.' Is this a just assessment of the two characters?

This question is more specific than our sample question on Becky. It is looking for a general interpretation of the characters concerned, but also for some specific factual information about their activities in the novel—in this case, the simple fact that both Amelia and Dobbin do act selfishly at times. A good answer must contain this fact, but will go on to raise other points, for instance the general issue of the prevalence of selfishness in *Vanity Fair*.

Here is a brief sample essay which defends the depiction of Amelia and Dobbin:

QUALIFIED GOODNESS

To say that Amelia and Dobbin in *Vanity Fair* are too good to be believable is unfair. Thackeray gives both characters traits which show that even they have not escaped the prevailing human vice in the novel—egotism.

This is particularly true of Amelia. We may initially think that she is too good to be true, but one of Thackeray's triumphs in *Vanity Fair* is to lead us to re-evaluate our opinion of her. By the end of the novel, we realise that her supposedly selfless devotion to the memory of her husband actually involves the worst kind of selfishness—the heartless manipulation of another human being. It provides the excuse which allows her to accept Dobbin's love and devotion without giving anything in return.

Dobbin's faults are less obvious than Amelia's, yet even he is not perfectly good. Egotism creeps into his actions when he hurries on George's marriage, partly to spare Amelia's feelings, but also to avoid the torture of seeing her remain unmarried yet unattainable. By including this weakness in the noble and usually selfless Dobbin, Thackeray makes him a believable character in a fictional world in which self-interest is the ruling passion.

'The problem with Thackeray's characters is that they are incapable of growth.' Discuss.

Again, specific factual information is required here. It is worth pointing out that while most of the characters in *Vanity Fair* do not grow but simply adapt their basic personalities to new conditions, Rawdon Crawley does seem to grow. You might further show that this general lack of growth is not necessarily a 'problem,' though it is a just *description* of the novel. Much of the fun of reading *Vanity Fair* comes from seeing the way in which a character like Becky does indeed adapt herself to different situations instead of really changing. And Thackeray's more serious purpose of dramatising the vanity of our wishes and reminding us of our human frailty implies that human beings share certain weaknesses and illusions, which they cannot simply outgrow.

QUESTIONS ON NARRATIVE TECHNIQUE

The intrusive narrator

'Thackeray's best character is his narrator.' Do you agree? Discuss the ways in which the narrator makes his presence felt in Vanity Fair, or 'Vanity Fair would be a great novel if only the narrator would keep more in the background.' Discuss.

Both of these questions are centred on the same topic, which they view in opposite ways. You could respond to either question with the following thesis: 'The positive virtues of Thackeray's narrator more than outweigh any lack of dramatic vividness he may cause.' An argument even more favourable to the narrator would be: 'Thackeray's narrator makes the great scenes in *Vanity Fair* more vivid, not less vivid, because of the way he involves us in the world Thackeray has created.' In supporting either generalisation, you would give examples showing different ways in which the narrator makes himself felt in the novel, from long set addresses to the reader, to single words.

If you believe that the narrator is indeed more obtrusive than he ought to be, your task would be to prove your point by showing how his presence harms specific scenes in the novel.

QUESTIONS ON THE WORLD OF *VANITY FAIR*

Cynic or sentimentalist?

Thackeray has been described as part cynic, part sentimentalist. Is he either, or both, or neither?

This is a classic question on *Vanity Fair*. It raises the familiar contrast between Becky (who is often said to be cynically presented since she reflects a negative view of human beings) and Amelia (who is often supposed to be sentimentally portrayed since Thackeray appears to admire her excessively and uncritically). The issues raised by the two heroines have been discussed in the Commentary (page 62). Thackeray seems to the present author to be more cynical than sentimental, and more a pessimistic moralist than either. No matter what your own view, you need not only to discuss the two heroines in answering this question, but also to mention other characters in the novel. 'Good' characters such as Briggs or Lady Jane and 'wicked' characters such as Lord Steyne or Sir Pitt Crawley might be helpful. Thackeray's views concerning human selfishness are germane here. The depiction of children in the novel is also interesting. Thackeray has few illusions about their selfishness, yet he also tends to think of at least some of them (young Rawdon, for instance) as 'purer' than adults.

Here is an example of one way to approach the question:

CYNICAL SENTIMENTALISM

Is Thackeray a cynic or a sentimentalist? Surely he is the former. His treatment of character after character in *Vanity Fair* implies that individual men and women are ultimately selfish, and that the worst qualities of human nature are the ones which succeed in the world.

It is easy enough to find examples of Thackeray's cynicism. Lord Steyne, rich and publicly revered, is a dissolute man interested only in exercising his power and following his pleasures. In the very scene in which we see him bully and humiliate his wife and his daughter-in-law, Thackeray's cynical narrative voice reminds us of how delighted society is in his gracious behaviour towards them in public. The Crawley family also presents example after example of human weakness, folly, and injustice. One thinks of Sir Pitt's last days, maltreated by one of his own servants and whimpering like a baby.

Thackeray's cynicism undercuts even the sentimental aspects of the novel. His good characters are not entirely good, and the virtues they do possess render them victims of society. Even his sentimental attitude toward children is ironically undercut. Young George's schoolboy essay on selfishness describes a vice he himself exemplifies. In scenes where Thackeray's sentimentalism is not undercut, we can feel the presence of his cynicism in another way. He indulges in a sentimental adoration of weak women or small children as a means of escaping for the moment from a view of the world too bitter to be constantly endured.

Thackeray's views of society and life

'Thackeray succeeds as a critic of society, but he fails as a critic of life.' Discuss.

This question invites us to see Thackeray primarily as a social critic, and implies that there may be a large gap between criticising society and criticising life. To respond to the question, it is necessary to decide whether one agrees with either of these ideas. We have already argued that Thackeray is a great social critic and satirist, but that ultimately he is concerned with the vanity of human wishes in any human society. Some readers may feel, however, that Thackeray's view of human beings is too completely negative to be either accurate or helpful as a vision of life, though its very bleakness makes for effective satire on society.

If you hold the former view, you might frame the following thesis: 'Thackeray's satirical portrait of society is brilliant in itself, but it is only a means to his ultimate goal, which is to show us that man by his very nature always strives for things which, even if he achieves them, prove to be hollow.' The first part of the essay might give examples of the brilliance of Thackeray's social satire, such as his portrait of the 'Arcadian simplicity' at Queen's Crawley, or his picture of the Osborne household, or the chapters which describe Lord Steyne and his milieu. The essay could conclude by showing how all these individual scenes are in different ways examples of the vanity of human wishes.

The following sample answer discusses Lord Steyne. A full answer would give other examples as well.

THACKERAY AS A CRITIC OF SOCIETY AND LIFE

Thackeray's satirical portrait of society in *Vanity Fair* is brilliant in itself, but it is only a means to his ultimate goal, which is to show us that man always strives for things which, even if he achieves them, prove to be hollow. His picture of Lord Steyne and his family is a case in point. Steyne's long obituary, which lists line after line of honours, effectively satirises society for respecting unworthy men merely because of their wealth and power, but it also provides a larger comment on life. Lord Steyne possesses everything that ought to make one happy. He has power, social prominence, and wealth. Yet by the end of his days he is unable to enjoy the pleasures to which he devotes himself, and he constantly fears that he will be the next victim of the hereditary madness that lurks in his family. When we think of Lord Steyne, we may well ask with the narrator at the end of the novel: 'Which of us is happy in this world? Which of us has his desire? or, having it, is satisfied?'

Scenes for special study

If you were to be examined on the works of a poet, it would be wise to memorise a group of representative poems. With works as long and diffuse as novels, different tactics are required. Perhaps the most helpful thing you can do to prepare for an examination is to pick the scenes which you find most important in the novel, think carefully about their full significance, and make sure that you have their details clearly in mind. Here is a list of some of the scenes which are likely to be useful as evidence in answering a large number of different questions. Try to add some scenes from *Vanity Fair* which stand out in your own mind: fresh examples are always welcome in essays.

1. Becky and Amelia leave school (Chapter 1)

   A favourite examination question asks the student to discuss the opening chapter of a given novel. In the summary of Chapters 1 and 2, the significance of the opening scene in *Vanity Fair* has been discussed in considerable, though not exhaustive, detail

2. Sir Pitt proposes to Becky (Chapter 14)

3. Mr Osborne takes down the family Bible (Chapter 24)

4. Rawdon discovers Becky and Lord Steyne together when he returns home from the sponging-house (Chapter 53)

5. Dobbin tells Amelia that she is not worthy of him (Chapter 66)

6. Dobbin and Amelia see Becky at the charity bazaar (Chapter 67)

Part 5

Suggestions for further reading

The text

Two carefully annotated, reliably edited texts of *Vanity Fair* with good introductions are at present available in paperback, one edited by J.I.M. Stewart, Penguin Books, Harmondsworth, 1968, the other edited by Geoffrey and Kathleen Tillotson, Houghton Mifflin, Boston, 1963. The Tillotson edition contains all of Thackeray's full-page illustrations and a few of his smaller drawings. The Stewart edition has only one of Thackeray's drawings; on the other hand, its notes are very full. For a look at all of Thackeray's drawings, the student will need to consult one of the complete editions of Thackeray, for instance the Oxford Thackeray, edited by George Saintsbury, 1908.

Books about Thackeray

HARDY, BARBARA: *The Exposure of Luxury: Radical Themes in Thackeray*. Peter Owen, London, 1972. A more measured approach to social criticism in Thackeray's novel than that of Arnold Kettle and Dorothy Van Ghent.

KETTLE, ARNOLD: *An Introduction to the English Novel*, second edition, 2 vols, Hutchinson, London, 1967. This argues that the novel is aesthetically and morally incoherent.

LUBBOCK, PERCY: *The Craft of Fiction*, Jonathan Cape, London, 1921. This contains the classic statement of the view that the narrator of *Vanity Fair* is too intrusive.

McMASTER, JULIET: *Thackeray: The Major Novels*, Manchester University Press, Manchester, 1971.This is the best recent introduction to the novel, and is particularly good on the narrator and on the novel as a moral education for the reader.

RAY, GORDON N.: *Thackeray: The Uses of Adversity*, McGraw Hill, New York, 1955, and *Thackeray: The Age of Wisdom*, McGraw Hill, New York, 1958. This two-volume work is the standard life of Thackeray.

RAY, GORDON N.: *The Buried Life: A Study of the Relations between Thackeray's Fiction and his Personal History*, Oxford University Press, London, 1952. A particularly useful short study which concentrates entirely on the relation between Thackeray's life and his fiction.

TILLOTSON, GEOFFREY: *Thackeray the Novelist*, corrected edition, Methuen, London, 1963. A valuable, extended discussion of Thackeray's different voices.

TILLOTSON, KATHLEEN: *Novels of the Eighteen-Forties*, Oxford University Press, London, 1961. Gives a good discussion of the unity of *Vanity Fair* and describes the literary milieu in which Thackeray worked.

VAN GHENT, DOROTHY: *The English Novel: Form and Function*, Rinehart, New York, 1953; Harper, New York, 1961. Another view of *Vanity Fair* as an unsuccessful critique of nineteenth-century capitalism.

The author of these notes

HARRY EDMUND SHAW was educated at Harvard University and the University of California, Berkeley. He held an English-Speaking Union Schoolboy Fellowship at Winchester College, Hampshire, England, and spent a year as a Fulbright Scholar at the University of Edinburgh in Scotland. At present, he teaches English at Cornell University and is writing a book about historical fiction.

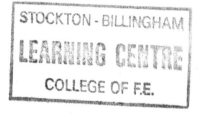